THE BOOK OF

MEDITERRANEAN
COOKING

LESLEY MACKLEY

Photographed by
SIMON BUTCHER

HPBooks

ANOTHER BEST SELLING VOLUME FROM HPBOOKS

HPBooks
Published by The Berkley Publishing Group
200 Madison Avenue
New York, NY 10016

9 8 7 6 5 4 3 2 1

ISBN 1-55788-244-4

First United States Printing ~ February 1996

By arrangement with Salamander Books Ltd.

Food Stylist: Nicola Fowler
Printed in Belgium by Proost International Book Production

CONTENTS

FOREWORD

Whether in Europe, Africa or Asia, the countries that surround the Mediterranean Sea have a rich tradition of fine food that is at last being discovered all over the world, as much for health reasons as for its varied range of delicious dishes. The Mediterranean diet has changed little over the centuries yet is ideally suited to modern-day living. It has always been naturally healthy: foods are cooked in olive oil rather than butter, and meats and dairy produce are of secondary importance, replaced by the abundant supplies of fish and seafood and the fresh fruits and vegetables that grow so well in the warm, sunny climate.

This mouthwatering collection of recipes shows you how to make the most of the traditional Mediterranean ingredients that are now widely available in our supermarkets. From Seafood Paella to Tuscan Tomato Soup, Basque Chicken to Fruit and Nut Baklava, the authentic dishes in this book offer the ideal introduction to the cuisine of this fascinating area.

MEDITERRANEAN CUISINE

Some fifteen countries, spanning three continents, border the Mediterranean Sea, not to mention the scores of islands dotted throughout its waters. The area to the north includes southern Spain and France, Italy, Greece and Turkey; to the east is Syria, Lebanon and Israel; along the southern shores lie Morocco, Algeria, Tunisia and Egypt. To categorize the food and cooking of all these countries under one heading may seem ambitious, and each one is rightly proud of its individuality, but they have a surprising amount in common and a Mediterranean theme can be seen throughout.

Climate and landscape vary little throughout the area, and it is these factors that determine the similar characteristics of all the Mediterranean cuisines. Every country relies heavily on the sea for its fish and seafood. Fruits and vegetables grow very well, as do cereals, but poor pastures mean a lack of dairy products and a shortage of beef. Any major differences in the eating habits of the Mediterranean countries are mainly due to religious variations, such as taboos on eating pork and shellfish.

The basic Mediterranean diet of antiquity consisted of olives, wheat, figs and grapes. The turbulent history of the Mediterranean and the constant movement of its peoples led to a great interchange of customs, including eating habits. In addition, the traffic of cargo ships, stopping frequently to load and unload, resulted in the introduction of foods from other countries. Oranges and lemons came from China, eggplant from Southeast Asia, spinach from Persia and okra from Africa, while tomatoes, peppers, corn, squashes and beans arrived from the New World in the sixteenth century.

THE MEDITERRANEAN DIET

It is now widely recognized that the Mediterranean diet is one of the healthiest in the world. It is low in processed foods and animal fats and is based on fresh produce, particularly wheat, fresh fruit and vegetables and olive oil. As our supermarkets and delicatessens stock a broader range of these ingredients, a Mediterranean diet is now accessible to all of us.

MEAT

Meat does not have the significance it has in North America and has always been a comparative luxury around the Mediterranean. Sheep and goats, which are the only animals that survive well on the poor pastures, tend to

Left to right, from top: Grey mullet, squid, red mullet, sea bass, Mediterranean shrimp, mussels, scallops, sardines, tuna steaks.

Left to right, from top: Oak leaf lettuce, leeks, onions, yellow and red bell peppers, Belgian endive, baby globe artichokes, eggplant, zucchini, fennel, chile peppers, vine tomatoes, okra, garlic, beefsteak tomato.

produce tough, strongly flavored meat, so techniques such as marinating and long, slow cooking are used to make them tender. On special occasions, however, a whole young lamb may be spit-roasted. Beef from mature animals is rare as it is almost impossible to fatten calves to maturity; they are more often eaten as veal. Pork is usually cured and made into ham or sausages.

POULTRY AND GAME
The first mention of poultry-keeping in Europe is in a Greek document of 570 BC, and poultry and game, especially chicken, are still as popular as ever. Guinea fowl, partridge, pheasant and quail, as well as rabbit and hare, frequently appear in traditional recipes.

DAIRY PRODUCE
Sheep and goats have always been the main dairy animals of the area around the Mediterranean. Cow milk is becoming more common, but milk is still not very popular as a drink. In the days before refrigeration it had to be made into longer lasting products such as cheese and yogurt. Yogurt is particularly widely used in Turkey and Greece, and Greek-style yogurt, made from sheep or cow milk, is now more widely available. It is a thick, drained yogurt with a slightly sweet flavor. If possible, use it whenever a recipe in

this book includes yogurt. In southern Italy buffaloes, descended from animals introduced from India, provide milk that has a high fat content, most of which is made into high quality (and expensive) mozzarella cheese.

FISH AND SHELLFISH
Fish and shellfish have always played a very important part in the Mediterranean diet and, as anybody who has visited a Mediterranean fish market will agree, the variety to be found in these waters is staggering. In spite of worries that pollution and over-fishing may be spoiling this natural bounty, seafood is still widely eaten. Red and gray mullet are very popular, as are turbot, bass, sea bream, swordfish, tuna, sardines, monkfish and shellfish such as scallops, crab, mussels, shrimp and lobster. The most common method of cooking is grilling over charcoal, but seafood soups and stews are also popular - each country has its own specialty. Octopus and squid, which are tenderized by being beaten against stones, are usually served fried, grilled or cooked in a sauce. Fresh anchovies are found all around the area, but are more widely sold preserved in oil. They are an essential ingredient in many Italian meals and in dishes from southern France such as salade niçoise, anchoïade and tapénade.

*Left to right, from top: Lemons, pears, plums, pomegranates,
oranges, figs, grapes and vine leaves, charentais melon, cherries,
dates, apricots, peaches.*

VEGETABLES

Vegetables grow well in the warm, sunny climate and are an important part of the Mediterranean diet. They frequently feature as a dish in their own right rather than as an accompaniment. Red, green and yellow bell peppers, chile peppers, tomatoes, zucchini, eggplant, onions and garlic grow in abundance and feature in similar ways in many Mediterranean recipes. Other popular vegetables include spinach, artichokes, fava beans, green beans, fennel, leeks and okra.

FRUIT

The fruits of the Mediterranean can be found in all kinds of dishes, both sweet and savory. The high quality of the local produce means it needs little preparation and a simple bowl of fresh, ripe fruit is often served in place of a more elaborate dessert.

Citrus fruits grow particularly well, and lemons and oranges are important features of the cuisines of Greece, Turkey, Morocco and Israel, being used to flavor everything from soups and sauces to cakes and pastries. Lemon juice is squeezed on meat, poultry or fish to add flavor before grilling and to act as a tenderizer. Whole preserved lemons add a distinctive flavor to many North African stews. Apricots, cherries, dates, figs, melons, plums, peaches and pomegranates also flourish. Many fruits are dried, including apricots, dates, figs, plums and peaches, and are frequently used in Middle Eastern cooking, where they add a little sweetness to meat dishes.

The vine and the olive tree have always played a vital role in the life of Mediterranean countries. The extent of the Mediterranean area to the north is often defined as being the limit of fruiting olive trees. Olives come in all shapes and sizes, the largest being the queen olives grown in Spain and the smallest the tiny ripe olives from Nice. A huge variety of olive oil is now available and the range can be confusing. A good quality blended oil is suitable for most cooked dishes, but for salad dressings or drizzling over pasta, a fruity, extra-virgin oil gives a superior flavor.

Extensive vineyards produce grapes for making wine as well as dessert grapes, and even the leaves of the vine are eaten - either stuffed to make dolmades, or wrapped around food such as fish to keep it moist and add flavor during grilling.

NUTS

Nuts are grown throughout the Mediterranean, many for export. The best walnuts are grown in Italy, France and Turkey, while Italy is also a renowned producer of hazelnuts. Almonds are popular in many sweet dishes and pastries, and in the Middle East they are also used in savory dishes such as pilafs. Ground almonds are often used for thickening sauces and soups. Pine nuts are frequently added to sweet and savory dishes from Spain to the Middle East and are essential in the pesto sauce of Italy and the pistou of Provence. Bright green pistachio nuts feature in many Middle Eastern and Italian dishes.

HERBS AND SPICES

Herbs are widely used on the northern shores of the Mediterranean, particularly France, while spices are more prevalent in the south. Basil and oregano are vital ingredients in many Italian dishes. In the Middle Eastern countries parsley and mint are used in vast quantities - mint is often dried to give it a more intense flavor. Cilantro is another popular herb all over the area.

Along the North African shores, spices such as cinnamon, ground coriander and cumin appear in many dishes to give a fragrant spicy flavor without heat. Saffron is an essential ingredient in fish dishes, Italian risottos and Moroccan couscous. It is the most expensive spice in the world, but providing you use good-quality saffron (preferably strands rather than powder) a little goes a long way.

Harissa, the fiery paste made from pounded chiles, is an important ingredient in many North African dishes. It is very hot, so be sure to use it in moderation. Other popular flavorings include rose water (the distinctive flavoring of Turkish delight) and orange flower water. Both need only be used in small amounts to add fragrance and flavor to a dish.

BEANS AND GRAINS

Many legumes, such as fava beans, chickpeas, haricot beans and kidney beans, are dried for use during the winter months. They feature in many of the area's salads, soups and stews.

Wheat is one of the main crops grown around the Mediterranean. The most common type is a hard durum wheat, high in gluten and ideal for making pasta, pastry and bread - from the pitta bread to baguettes, bread has always been a very important part of a Mediterranean meal. Wheat also provides semolina for making couscous. Bulghur wheat is a form of cracked wheat popular in Middle Eastern countries.

Secondary cereal crops include rice and corn. Short-grain rice, grown in Spain, Italy and Egypt, is the main ingredient for Spanish paellas, Italian risottos, Turkish pilafs and many Middle Eastern dishes. Corn, grown extensively near Venice, is eaten throughout Italy as polenta.

Left, to right, from top: Pitta bread, French country bread, small baguette, lavender, bulghur wheat, spaghetti, couscous, cinnamon sticks, flat-leaf parsley, basil, coriander seeds, cumin seeds, bay leaves, oregano, mint, cilantro, short-grain rice, harissa, walnuts, hazelnuts, almonds.

CASCADILLA

1 lb. ripe tomatoes, peeled (page 17)
1/2 cucumber
1 green bell pepper
2 green onions
1 garlic clove, crushed
1 teaspoon honey
2 teaspoons chopped fresh tarragon
1 cup tomato juice, chilled
1 tablespoon balsamic vinegar
1-1/4 cups regular plain yogurt, refrigerated
Salt and freshly ground pepper
Green onion slices and chopped fresh parsley, to
  garnish

Cut tomatoes into quarters, remove seeds and roughly chop flesh.

Cut cucumber lengthwise into quarters and remove seeds. Roughly chop flesh. Cut bell pepper into quarters and remove core and seeds. Roughly chop green onions.

Put green onions into a food processor or blender with tomatoes, cucumber, bell pepper, garlic, honey, tarragon, tomato juice and vinegar. Process until well blended. Transfer to a bowl. Stir in yogurt and season with salt and pepper. Refrigerate 1 hour. Garnish with green onion slices and chopped parsley and serve.

Makes 4 servings.

SOUPE AU PISTOU

1/2 cup dried haricot beans, soaked overnight
1/4 cup olive oil
1 onion, chopped
2 leeks, white parts only, chopped
1 carrot, diced
2 stalks celery, thinly sliced
4-1/2 cups vegetable stock
4oz. shelled broad beans or lima beans
6oz. green beans, cut into short lengths
2 zucchini, diced
3 tomatoes, peeled (page 17), seeded and chopped
Salt and freshly ground pepper
3 tablespoons pesto sauce
Parmesan cheese, to serve

Drain haricot beans and put into a large saucepan. Cover with cold water and bring to a boil. Boil rapidly 10 minutes, then cover and simmer 30 minutes. Drain. Heat oil in a saucepan. Add onion, leeks, carrot and celery. Cook 5 minutes or until beginning to soften.

Add stock and haricot beans. Cover and simmer 30 to 40 minutes or until beans are tender. Add broad beans or lima beans, green beans, zucchini and tomatoes and cook 10 minutes or until all vegetables are tender. Season with salt and pepper. Stir in pesto. Use a vegetable peeler to shave Parmesan cheese on to soup and serve.

Makes 6 to 8 servings.

BOUILLABAISSE

2-1/4 lbs. mixed fish fillets and shellfish (red mullet, monkfish, raw shrimp, mussels)
3 tablespoons olive oil
1 onion, chopped
1 leek, sliced
1 stalk celery, chopped
2 garlic cloves, crushed
4 ripe tomatoes, peeled (page 17) and chopped
1/2 teaspoon dried herbes de Provence
2 strips pared orange zest
Large pinch of saffron strands
Salt and freshly ground pepper
2/3 cup dry white wine
2-1/3 cups good fish stock
Chopped fresh parsley, to garnish

Skin fish and remove any bones. Cut into chunks. Heat oil in a large saucepan. Add onion, leek, celery and garlic and cook over low heat 5 minutes or until soft. Add tomatoes, herbes de Provence, orange zest, saffron, salt and pepper. Add wine and stock and bring to a boil.

Reduce heat, add firmest fish and simmer 5 minutes. Add more delicate fish and shellfish. Cover and simmer 5 minutes or until fish is cooked through but still retains its shape and mussels have opened. Discard any mussels that have not opened. Garnish with chopped parsley and serve.

Makes 6 servings.

Note: Use fish and shellfish trimmings to make stock.

FENNEL & LEMON SOUP

2 tablespoons olive oil
1 onion, roughly chopped
2 fennel bulbs, thinly sliced
2-1/2 cups chicken stock
Grated zest of 1 lemon
2/3 to 1-1/4 cups milk
Salt and freshly ground pepper
Fennel leaves, to garnish
FRIED LEMON ZEST:
1 lemon
Vegetable oil for frying

To make fried lemon zest, use a lemon zester to take as many strips of zest as possible from lemon.

Squeeze lemon into a small bowl and add zest to juice. Leave 1 hour then drain. Dry lemon zest on paper towels. Heat 1/2 inch oil in a small saucepan. Add zest and fry a few seconds until beginning to color. Remove with a slotted spoon and set aside.

Heat olive oil in a large saucepan. Add onion and cook over low heat 5 minutes or until soft. Stir in fennel slices. Add stock and grated lemon zest and bring to a boil. Reduce heat, cover and simmer 20 minutes or until fennel is tender. Transfer to a food processor or blender and process until smooth. Add enough milk to give desired consistency and season with salt and pepper. Garnish with fried lemon zest and fennel leaves and serve hot or chilled.

Makes 4 servings.

── GARLIC & ALMOND SOUP ──

2 garlic cloves, chopped
1 cup ground almonds
1 cup fresh bread crumbs
2 tablespoons olive oil
1 tablespoon white wine vinegar
Salt and freshly ground pepper
4oz. seedless green grapes
2 teaspoons chopped fresh cilantro

Put garlic in a food processor or blender with ground almonds and bread crumbs.

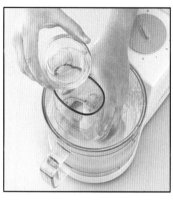

Measure 2-1/2 cups cold water into a measuring cup. Add a little of water to bread crumb mixture and process to form a paste. With motor running, gradually pour in oil, vinegar and remaining water.

Transfer to a bowl, season with salt and pepper and refrigerate at least 1 hour. Whisk soup and adjust seasoning. Halve grapes and stir into soup with cilantro. Serve in refrigerated bowls.

Makes 4 servings.

TUSCAN TOMATO SOUP

2 tablespoons olive oil
1 small onion, finely chopped
1 leek, finely chopped
2 garlic cloves, crushed
1-1/2 lbs. ripe plum tomatoes
3-3/4 cups chicken stock
2 teaspoons tomato paste
Salt and freshly ground black pepper
Pinch of sugar (optional)
1/2 ciabatta loaf, crusts removed
12 basil leaves, shredded
Extra-virgin olive oil, to serve

Heat oil in a large saucepan. Add onion, leek and garlic. Cook over low heat until soft.

Put tomatoes in a bowl. Cover with boiling water and leave 1 minute. Pour off water and cover tomatoes with cold water. Leave 1 minute. Peel tomatoes and chop roughly. Add to saucepan. Stir in chicken stock, tomato paste, salt and pepper and a little sugar, if desired. Bring to a boil, reduce heat, cover and simmer 30 minutes.

Just before serving, break bread into bite-size pieces and divide among four warmed serving bowls. Stir basil into soup and ladle soup over bread. Drizzle with a little extra-virgin olive oil and serve.

Makes 4 to 6 servings.

Note: Adding a pinch of sugar to soup brings out the flavor of the tomatoes.

—— PROVENÇAL FISH SOUP ——

2 tablespoons olive oil
1 leek, sliced
2 stalks celery, chopped
1 onion, chopped
2 garlic cloves, chopped
4 ripe tomatoes, chopped
1 tablespoon tomato paste
2/3 cup dry white wine
Bouquet garni
1 teaspoon saffron strands
2-1/4lbs. mixed fish fillets and shellfish, fish
   trimmings, bones and heads
Salt and freshly ground pepper
Croûtons and shredded Gruyère cheese, to serve
ROUILLE:
1 slice white bread, crusts removed
1 red bell pepper
1 or 2 fresh red chiles, seeded and chopped
2 garlic cloves, crushed
Olive oil

To make rouille, soak bread in cold water 10 minutes then squeeze dry. Preheat broiler. Quarter bell pepper and remove core and seeds. Broil, skin side up, until skin is charred and blistered. Put into a plastic bag and leave until cool enough to handle. Peel off skin.

Roughly chop bell pepper and put in a food processor or blender with bread, chiles and garlic. Process, adding a little olive oil, if necessary, to form a coarse paste. Transfer to a small bowl and set aside.

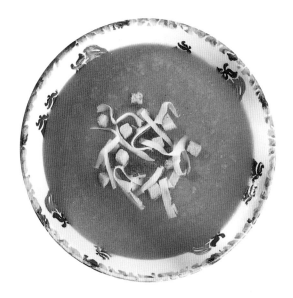

Heat olive oil in a large saucepan. Add leek, celery, onion and garlic. Cook over low heat 10 minutes or until soft. Add tomatoes, tomato paste, wine, bouquet garni, saffron, any shellfish and fish trimmings. Bring to a boil, reduce heat, cover and simmer 30 minutes.

Strain through a colander into a clean saucepan, pressing out as much liquid as possible. Discard shellfish, trimmings and vegetables. Cut fish fillets into large chunks and add to strained soup. Cover and simmer 10 minutes or until fish is cooked through. Strain through a colander into a clean saucepan. Put cooked fish in a food processor or blender with 1-1/4 cups of soup. Process until well blended but still retaining some texture.

Stir fish back into remaining soup. Season and reheat gently. Serve soup with rouille, croûtons and grated cheese handed separately.

Makes 4 to 6 servings.

Note: The fish and shellfish mixture should contain white fish fillets, a small piece of smoked cod and a few mussels and shrimp.

ASPARAGUS NIÇOISE

1 tablespoon lemon juice
1 lb. asparagus spears
8 oz. cherry tomatoes, halved
12 black olives, pitted and halved
Basil sprigs, to garnish
DRESSING:
1 teaspoon Dijon mustard
1 tablespoon white wine vinegar
Salt and freshly ground pepper
1/3 cup extra-virgin olive oil
1 hard-cooked egg, finely chopped

Add lemon juice to a saucepan of boiling salted water. Snap tough ends from asparagus. Tie spears in a bundle.

Stand bundle upright in pan so that tips stand out of water. Cover with a dome of foil and simmer 10 minutes or until tender. Drain well and let cool. Take 16 stalks and cut in half lengthwise, cutting as far as bottom of tip so that tip remains intact. Cut remaining stalks into 1-inch lengths and put in a bowl with tomatoes and olives.

Arrange four asparagus spears on each of four serving plates to make a square, with a tip at each corner and halved stalks splayed out at right angles. To make dressing, whisk together mustard, vinegar, salt and pepper then whisk in oil. Stir in chopped hard-cooked egg. Pour dressing over tomato and asparagus mixture and toss together. Arrange mixture in center of asparagus squares. Garnish with basil sprigs and serve.

Makes 4 servings.

TAPÉNADE

4oz. black olives
3 tablespoons capers
1 (2-oz.) can anchovies in olive oil, drained
1 garlic clove, chopped
1 tablespoon lemon juice
1 teaspoon Dijon mustard
Freshly ground pepper
1/2 cup olive oil
Hard-boiled eggs and toasted French bread, to serve
Flat-leaf parsley sprigs, to garnish

Remove pits from olives and put olives in a food processor or blender.

Add capers, anchovies, garlic, lemon juice, mustard and black pepper. Process until roughly blended. With motor running, slowly pour in olive oil to form a thick, slightly grainy paste.

Mix some of tapénade with yolks of hard-cooked eggs, in equal quantities, and pile back into whites. Spread remaining tapénade on toasted bread. Garnish with flat-leaf parsley and serve.

Makes 4 servings.

Note: Tapénade will keep well stored in an air-tight jar in refrigerator.

GREEK YOGURT DIP

1/2 cucumber
1 teaspoon salt
2/3 cup regular plain yogurt
1 garlic clove, crushed
1 tablespoon chopped fresh mint
1 tablespoon chopped fresh cilantro
Grated zest of 1/2 orange
1 teaspoon honey
Freshly ground pepper
Cucumber twists and mint and cilantro sprigs, to
  garnish
Crudités and pitta bread, to serve

Peel cucumber, cut lengthwise into quarters
and remove seeds.

Cut cucumber into small dice. Put into a
colander, sprinkle with salt and leave 30
minutes. Pat dry with paper towels.

In a bowl, mix together cucumber, yogurt,
garlic, mint, cilantro, orange zest, honey and
black pepper. Transfer to a serving bowl.
Garnish with cucumber twists, mint and
cilantro and serve at once, with crudités and
pitta bread.

Makes 4 servings.

EGGPLANT ROLLS

2 eggplants, each weighing 8oz.
3 tablespoons olive oil
4oz. mozzarella cheese, diced
2 tomatoes, peeled (page 17), seeded and diced
1 tablespoon chopped fresh basil
Salt and freshly ground pepper
Basil sprigs, to garnish
RED BELL PEPPER SAUCE:
1 tablespoon olive oil
1 small onion, chopped
2 red bell peppers, diced
3/4 cup vegetable stock

To make red bell pepper sauce, heat oil in a saucepan. Add onion and cook over low heat 5 minutes or until soft. Add bell peppers and cook over low heat 5 minutes. Pour in stock, bring to a boil, reduce heat and simmer 10 minutes. Transfer to a food processor or blender and process until smooth. Press through a sieve into a bowl. Season with salt and pepper and set aside. Cut each eggplant lengthwise into eight 1/4-inch slices. Preheat oven to 375F (190C). Preheat broiler.

Brush eggplant slices on both sides with oil then broil, turning once, until soft and beginning to brown. Mix together mozzarella cheese, tomatoes, basil, salt and pepper. Put a little on one end of each eggplant slice and roll up. Put rolls, seam side down, in an ovenproof dish. Cook in oven 10 to 15 minutes. Reheat sauce. Arrange four rolls on each plate, garnish with basil sprigs and serve with red bell pepper sauce.

Makes 4 servings.

HUMMUS

2 teaspoons cumin seeds
1 (15-oz.) can chickpeas, drained
1/4 cup ground almonds
1 garlic clove, crushed
2/3 cup regular plain yogurt
1 tablespoon olive oil
2 teaspoons chopped fresh mint
Juice of 1/2 lemon
Salt and freshly ground pepper
Olive oil and cayenne pepper, to garnish
Crudités and pitta bread, to serve

Heat a small heavy skillet and add cumin seeds. Dry fry, shaking pan, until seeds begin to smell aromatic.

Reserve a few cumin seeds for garnish and put remainder in a food processor or blender. Add chickpeas, ground almonds, garlic, yogurt, olive oil, mint, lemon juice, salt and pepper. Process to form a slightly grainy paste.

Transfer to a serving dish and let stand 30 minutes. Drizzle with a little olive oil and sprinkle with cayenne pepper and reserved cumin seeds. Serve with crudités and fingers of pitta bread.

Makes 4 servings.

— MEDITERRANEAN FRITTATA —

3 tablespoons olive oil
1 small onion, thinly sliced
1 garlic clove, crushed
1 small red bell pepper, sliced
1 zucchini, thinly sliced
1 oz. sun-dried tomatoes, roughly chopped
2 oz. chorizo sausage, thinly sliced
4 eggs
1 teaspoon chopped fresh basil
Salt and freshly ground pepper
Red bell pepper rings and basil leaves, to garnish

Heat olive oil in a 8-inch omelet pan or skillet. Add onion and garlic and cook 2 minutes or until beginning to soften. Add bell pepper and zucchini and cook, stirring occasionally, until softened, but still retaining some 'bite'. Stir in sun-dried tomatoes and chorizo.

Beat eggs and add basil, salt and pepper. Pour eggs into pan and cook over a medium heat 6 to 8 minutes or until underside is browned and eggs are almost set. Preheat broiler. Put frittata under a medium broiler and broil 3 or 4 minutes or until eggs are set on top. Cut into wedges, garnish with bell pepper rings and basil leaves and serve warm or at room temperature.

Makes 2 to 4 servings.

——— SHRIMP & FETA PURSES ———

3 tablespoons butter, melted
4oz. cooked, peeled shrimp, thawed if frozen
6oz. feta cheese, crumbled
1oz. sun-dried tomatoes, roughly chopped
1 teaspoon chopped fresh chives
1 teaspoon chopped fresh fennel
Salt and freshly ground pepper
6 sheets filo pastry, about 16- x 12-inch
Fennel leaves and lemon twists, to garnish

Preheat oven to 400F (200C). Brush a baking sheet with melted butter. Dry shrimp on paper towels and roughly chop.

Mix together shrimp, feta cheese, sun-dried tomatoes, chives, fennel, salt and pepper. Cut each sheet of filo pastry into twelve squares. Brush each square with melted butter and layer three more squares on top, arranging them at different angles to form petals.

Place a spoonful of shrimp mixture in middle of pastry. Pull up edges of pastry and pinch together at top to form a purse. Put on baking sheet and brush with melted butter. Cook in oven 10 to 15 minutes or until golden brown. Garnish with fennel leaves and lemon twists and serve.

Makes 6 servings.

— TUNISIAN EGGS & PEPPERS —

2 tablespoons olive oil
1 onion, thinly sliced
1 red bell pepper, cut into strips
1 yellow bell pepper, cut into strips
1 fresh red chile, seeded and finely chopped
6 tomatoes, peeled (page 17) and quartered
Salt and freshly ground pepper
2 teaspoons chopped fresh mint
4 eggs
Mint sprigs, to garnish

Heat oil in a heavy skillet. Add onion and cook 5 minutes or until soft.

Add bell peppers and chile, cover and cook 8 minutes or until bell peppers are just tender. Preheat oven to 350F (180C). Add tomatoes to bell pepper mixture, cover and cook 5 to 8 minutes or until vegetables are blended but still retain their shape and texture. Season with salt and pepper and stir in mint.

Divide mixture among four ovenproof dishes. Make an indentation in vegetables and carefully add an egg to each one. Cook in oven 12 to 15 minutes or until eggs have set. Garnish with mint sprigs and serve.

Makes 4 servings.

Note: The eggs may be cooked in skillet, if preferred. Make four indentations in mixture and break in eggs. Cover and cook over low heat 5 minutes, basting occasionally with juices.

PAN BAGNAT

1/4 red and 1/4 green bell pepper
1 (2-oz.) can anchovies in olive oil
1/3 cup olive oil
1 garlic clove, crushed
1 tablespoon lemon juice
1 ciabatta loaf
3 ripe tomatoes, sliced
1/2 small red onion, thinly sliced
1 hard-cooked egg, thinly sliced
Salt and freshly ground pepper
6 black olives, pitted and roughly chopped
A few basil leaves

Preheat broiler. Broil bell peppers, skin side up, until charred and blistered.

Put bell peppers into a plastic bag and leave until cool enough to handle. Peel off skins. Remove core and seeds and slice flesh into thin strips. Drain anchovies, reserving oil. Roughly chop anchovies. Heat olive oil in a saucepan, add anchovies and their oil, garlic and lemon juice and heat gently, mashing anchovies until they have almost melted into sauce. Let cool.

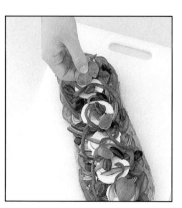

Cut ciabatta lengthwise in half. Brush each cut side with some of anchovy mixture. Layer tomatoes, onion, egg and bell pepper strips on one ciabatta half. Season with salt and pepper. Scatter with olives and basil leaves. Put other half of loaf on top. Press together and wrap tightly in plastic wrap. Put a weight on top and leave at least 1 hour. Cut into 8 to 10 slices and serve.

Makes 8 to 10 slices.

BROILED RADICCHIO

2 large heads of radicchio
6 anchovies in olive oil
2 garlic cloves, cut into slivers
1/3 cup olive oil
Salt and freshly ground pepper
4oz. mozzarella cheese, thinly sliced
Lemon slices, to garnish

Cut radicchio lengthwise in half. Drain anchovies, reserving oil, and chop.

Push garlic and anchovy pieces between radicchio leaves. Heat half olive oil in a flameproof dish. Put radicchio halves, cut side up, in dish and cook over low heat 5 minutes or until underside of radicchio softens and begins to brown. Remove from heat.

Preheat broiler. Season radicchio with salt and pepper. Drizzle with a little anchovy oil and remaining olive oil. Arrange mozzarella slices on top of radicchio and broil until mozzarella is bubbling and beginning to brown. Garnish with lemon slices and serve immediately.

Makes 4 servings.

BROILED GOAT CHEESE

4 small fresh goat cheeses or 4 slices from a log of
  goat cheese
Salt and freshly ground pepper
Sprig of thyme
Sprig of rosemary
1 fresh bay leaf
1 tablespoon brandy
1/3 cup extra-virgin olive oil
4 vacuum-packed vine leaves
Thyme sprigs, to garnish
Toasted French bread, to serve

Put goat cheese on a plate and season with
salt and pepper.

Put thyme, rosemary and bay leaf on top of
cheese then spoon brandy and most of olive
oil on top. Cover and leave in a cool place 2
or 3 hours, basting cheese occasionally. Rinse
vine leaves and dry on paper towels.

Preheat broiler. Put a piece of cheese on each
vine leaf and wrap leaves around cheese,
securing with a wooden cocktail stick. Brush
parcels with remaining olive oil and cook
under broiler or on a grill 3 or 4 minutes on
each side, until leaves are just charred. Open
up parcels slightly, garnish with thyme sprigs
and serve with toasted French bread.

Makes 4 servings.

MARINATED OLIVES

4 oz. green olives
2 thin lemon slices, quartered
2 teaspoons coriander seeds, lightly crushed
1 teaspoon dried mint
2 garlic cloves, crushed
Olive oil to cover
4 oz. black olives
1/4 red bell pepper, cut into strips
1 fresh red chile, cored seeded and cut into rings
Sprig of thyme

Put green olives in a preserving jar or screw-top jar. Add lemon slices.

Add coriander, mint and half garlic to jar. Cover with olive oil and seal jar. Put black olives in another jar. Add red bell pepper, chile, thyme and remaining garlic.

Cover with olive oil and seal jar. Leave to marinate at least 2 days before serving.

Makes 6 servings.

DOLMADES

7 oz. package vacuum-packed vine leaves
1/2 cup long grain rice
3 tablespoons olive oil
1 small onion, finely chopped
2 oz. pine nuts
1/4 cup raisins
2 tablespoons chopped fresh mint
1/4 teaspoon ground cinnamon
Salt and freshly ground pepper
2 tablespoons tomato paste
2 teaspoons lemon juice
Olive oil and lemon juice, to serve
Lemon slices and mint sprigs, to garnish

Rinse vine leaves and pat dry with paper towels.

Put rice into a saucepan of boiling salted water, cover and simmer 15 minutes or until rice is just tender. Drain and set aside. Heat 2 tablespoons of oil in a skillet. Add onion and cook over low heat 5 minutes or until soft. Add pine nuts and cook until lightly browned. Stir in raisins, mint, cinnamon, cooked rice, salt and pepper. Let cool. Take 20 vine leaves. Put a teaspoonful of rice mixture on each one. Fold over sides and roll up.

Line a large saucepan with any remaining vine leaves. Put dolmades side by side in pan, to fit tightly. Mix together 1-1/4 cups water, remaining olive oil, tomato paste and lemon juice. Pour into pan. Put a plate on top of dolmades, cover and simmer 1 hour until tender. Remove with a slotted spoon and arrange on serving plates. Drizzle with a little olive oil and lemon juice, garnish with lemon slices and mint and serve warm or cold.

Makes 20.

BRUSCHETTA

1 lb. ripe tomatoes, peeled (page 17)
4 green onions, sliced
3 sun-dried tomatoes, chopped
6 black olives, pitted and chopped
1 tablespoon chopped fresh basil
Salt and freshly ground pepper
8 thick slices ciabatta
4 teaspoons pesto
2 tablespoons extra-virgin olive oil
Basil sprigs, to garnish

Cut tomatoes into quarters, remove seeds and cut flesh into small dice.

In a bowl, mix together tomatoes, green onions, sun-dried tomatoes, olives, basil, salt and pepper. Toast slices of bread on both sides then spread a little pesto on one side of each slice.

Spoon tomato mixture on top of each slice of toast then drizzle with olive oil. Garnish with basil sprigs and serve.

Makes 4 servings.

BUCATINI SICILIANA

12 oz. bucatini
1/4 cup olive oil
1 onion, chopped
2 garlic cloves, chopped
2 teaspoons capers
2 tablespoons sun-dried tomato paste
4 teaspoons pine nuts
1/2 cup fresh bread crumbs
1 tablespoon chopped fresh parsley
2 teaspoons chopped black olives

Bring a large saucepan of salted water to a boil. Add pasta and cook according to package instructions until just tender.

Meanwhile, heat 3 tablespoons of oil in a skillet. Add onion and garlic and cook over low heat 5 minutes or until soft. Add capers, tomato paste, 1/3 cup of water from saucepan of pasta and heat gently. Heat remaining oil in a skillet. When hot, add pine nuts and bread crumbs and cook, stirring, until crisp and golden. Stir in parsley.

Drain pasta and return to pan. Add caper mixture and toss to coat. Transfer to a warmed serving dish, sprinkle with bread crumb mixture and chopped olives and serve immediately.

Makes 4 servings.

Note: Bucatini is a long, thin, tubular type of pasta. If it is unavailable, spaghetti can be used instead.

——— PASTA WITH BROCCOLI ———

1 lb. broccoli
12 oz. trumpet-shaped pasta, eg campanelle
1/3 cup olive oil
2 garlic cloves, finely chopped
6 anchovies in olive oil, drained and chopped
1/2 fresh red chile, cored, seeded and finely chopped
Salt and freshly ground pepper
Parmesan cheese, to serve

Divide broccoli into small flowerets and slice stalks. Bring a large saucepan of salted water to a boil, add broccoli flowerets and stalks and cook 3 to 5 minutes or until just tender.

Remove broccoli with a slotted spoon and drain on paper towels. Add pasta to broccoli cooking water and cook according to package instructions until just tender. Meanwhile, heat half oil in a large skillet, add garlic and anchovies and cook, stirring, 1 minute.

Add chile and cook 1 minute. Gently stir in broccoli and season with salt and pepper. Drain pasta and add to broccoli mixture. Stir in remaining olive oil and cook, stirring, 1 minute. Transfer to a warmed serving dish. Use a vegetable peeler to shave Parmesan cheese on top of pasta and serve.

Makes 4 servings.

─── BULGHUR WHEAT PILAFF ───

2/3 cup bulghur wheat
2/3 cup Puy lentils
2-inch piece cinnamon stick
1 fresh bay leaf
2 tablespoons olive oil
4 slices pancetta, cut into strips
1 onion, thinly sliced
1 garlic clove, crushed
2 tablespoons chopped fresh parsley
2 tablespoons chopped fresh cilantro
Salt and freshly ground pepper
Flat-leaf parsley and cilantro sprigs, to garnish

Put bulghur wheat in a bowl and cover with twice its volume of warm water. Leave 1 hour until tender.

Rinse lentils and put in a saucepan with cinnamon stick and bay leaf. Cover with cold water and bring to a boil. Simmer 20 to 30 minutes or until tender. Meanwhile, heat 1 tablespoon of oil in a skillet, add pancetta and cook until crisp. Remove with a slotted spoon and drain on paper towels. Add onion and garlic to pan and cook over low heat 10 minutes or until soft and golden brown.

Drain bulghur wheat thoroughly. Drain lentils and discard cinnamon and bay leaf. In a bowl, mix together bulghur wheat, lentils, pancetta, onion and garlic, remaining oil, parsley and cilantro. Season with salt and pepper. Serve at room temperature or reheat gently and serve warm, garnished with parsley and cilantro sprigs.

Makes 4 servings.

— ROASTED BELL PEPPER PIZZA —

1 tablespoon sun-dried tomato paste
2 large red and 1 large yellow bell pepper, peeled
   (page 28) and cut into strips
3 garlic cloves, finely chopped
1 tablespoon roughly chopped fresh parsley
Salt and freshly ground pepper
1 tablespoon olive oil
PIZZA DOUGH:
1-1/2 cups white bread flour
1/4 teaspoon salt
1 teaspoon fast-acting yeast
1 tablespoon olive oil

To make pizza dough, sift flour and salt into
a warmed bowl. Stir in yeast.

Make a well in center and stir in olive oil and
about 1/2 cup tepid water to form a soft
dough - you may need to add more water.
Turn on to a well-floured surface and knead
5 minutes or until smooth and elastic. Put in
an oiled bowl, cover and leave in a warm
place 1 hour until doubled in size. Turn on
to a floured surface and knead again 2 or 3
minutes.

Roll out dough to a circle approximately 10-
inch in diameter and put on a lightly oiled
baking sheet. Pinch up edges to form a rim.
Spread sun-dried tomato paste over dough.
Arrange bell pepper strips on top. Sprinkle
with chopped garlic and parsley and season
with salt and pepper. Leave 20 minutes.
Preheat oven to 400F (200C). Drizzle pizza
with oil and cook in oven 15 to 20 minutes.
Cut into wedges and serve.

Makes 2 to 4 servings.

EGGPLANT PIZZA

12 oz. eggplant
1 garlic clove, crushed
1 tablespoon lemon juice
1 tablespoon chopped fresh parsley
Salt and freshly ground pepper
1 quantity pizza dough (page 37)
12 oz. tomatoes, sliced
5 oz. chorizo sausage, sliced
4 oz. feta cheese, crumbled
1 tablespoon roughly chopped fresh oregano
1 tablespoon olive oil
Oregano leaves, to garnish

Preheat oven to 350F (180C). Pierce eggplant all over with a skewer and put on a baking sheet.

Cook in oven 30 minutes or until soft. Halve eggplant and scoop soft flesh into a bowl. Stir in garlic, lemon juice, parsley, salt and pepper and let cool. Roll out pizza dough to fit a 12- x 9-inch jelly roll pan. Put dough in pan and pinch up edges to form a rim. Spread eggplant puree over dough.

Arrange tomato slices on top and season with salt and pepper. Arrange chorizo over tomatoes. Sprinkle with feta cheese and oregano. Leave 15 minutes. Preheat oven to 400F (200C). Drizzle pizza with olive oil and cook in oven 20 minutes. Cut into squares, garnish with oregano leaves and serve.

Makes 12 squares.

Note: The eggplant puree can be made in advance. It also makes a delicious dip.

PISSALADIÈRE

3 tablespoons olive oil
2 lbs. onions, thinly sliced
2 garlic cloves, crushed
1 teaspoon each chopped fresh oregano, thyme and
   rosemary
Salt and freshly ground pepper
1 quantity pizza dough (page 37)
2 teaspoons tapénade (page 72)
1 (2-oz.) can anchovies in olive oil
12 black olives, pitted and halved
Oregano sprigs, to garnish

Heat oil in a large skillet. Add onions and garlic and cook over very low heat, stirring occasionally, 1 hour until very soft but only lightly browned. Stir in herbs, salt and pepper. Preheat oven to 400F (200C).

Divide dough into six pieces and roll each into a 5-inch round. Put on oiled baking sheets. Spread a little tapénade over each round, to within 1/2-inch of rim. Cover with onions. Drain anchovies, reserving oil, and arrange anchovies on top with olives. Drizzle with a little anchovy oil. Cook in oven 15 minutes. Garnish with oregano sprigs and serve hot.

Makes 6.

SUMMER RISOTTO

2 cups chicken stock
4 oz. sugar snap peas
4 oz. asparagus, cut into 2-inch lengths
4 oz. green beans, cut into 2-inch lengths
1/2 cup dry white wine
1 tablespoon olive oil
4 green onions, chopped
1 garlic clove, crushed
1-1/4 cups Arborio rice
4 sun-dried tomatoes in oil, drained
1/4 cup grated Pecorino cheese
2 oz. prosciutto, roughly chopped
Salt and freshly ground pepper
Pecorino shavings and basil sprigs, to garnish

Put stock in a saucepan and bring to a boil. Add sugar snap peas, asparagus and green beans and cook 3 minutes. Remove with a slotted spoon and set aside. Add wine to stock and bring to a simmer. Heat olive oil in a large saucepan. Add green onions and garlic and cook over low heat 5 minutes or until soft. Add rice and cook, stirring, 2 minutes. Add a ladleful of simmering stock and cook, stirring, until absorbed. Continue adding stock, a ladleful at a time, as it is absorbed, stirring frequently.

Roughly chop sun-dried tomatoes. When rice has been cooking 15 minutes, add sugar snap peas, asparagus, beans, tomatoes and any remaining stock. Cook, stirring, until rice is tender and creamy. Stir in grated Pecorino and prosciutto and season with salt and pepper. Garnish with Pecorino shavings and basil and serve.

Makes 4 servings.

Note: Pecorino is a hard cheese from Italy. Replace it with Parmesan if it is unavailable.

VEGETABLE COUSCOUS

3 tablespoons olive oil
1 onion, chopped
2 garlic cloves, crushed
1 teaspoon ground cumin
1 teaspoon paprika
1 (14-oz.) can tomatoes
1-1/4 cups vegetable stock
1 cinnamon stick
Pinch of saffron strands
4 baby eggplant, quartered
8 baby zucchini, trimmed
8 baby carrots
Salt
1 (15-oz.) can chickpeas, drained
6 oz. pitted prunes
1-2/3 cups couscous
3 tablespoons chopped fresh parsley
3 tablespoons chopped fresh cilantro
2 or 3 teaspoons harissa

Heat olive oil in a large saucepan. Add onion and garlic and cook over low heat 5 minutes or until soft. Add cumin and paprika and cook, stirring, 1 minute. Add tomatoes, stock, cinnamon, saffron, eggplant, zucchini and carrots. Season with salt. Bring to a boil, reduce heat, cover and cook 20 minutes or until vegetables are just tender.

Add chickpeas and prunes and cook 10 minutes. Meanwhile, put couscous in a bowl and cover generously with boiling water. Leave 10 minutes then drain thoroughly and fluff up with a fork. Stir parsley and cilantro into vegetables. Heap couscous on to a warmed serving plate. Remove vegetables with a slotted spoon and arrange on top. Spoon over a little sauce. Stir harissa into remaining sauce and serve separately.

Makes 4 servings.

———— BAKED BASQUE COD ————

3 tablespoons olive oil
1 small green bell pepper, diced
1 onion, finely chopped
2 tomatoes, peeled (page 17) and diced
1 garlic clove, crushed
2 teaspoons chopped fresh basil
4 cod fillets, skinned, each weighing 6 oz.
Juice of 1/2 lemon
Salt and freshly ground pepper
Lemon slices, to garnish

Preheat oven to 375F (190C). Brush four large squares of foil with a little oil.

Mix together bell pepper, onion, tomatoes, garlic and basil. Put a cod fillet on each piece of foil. Top each fillet with bell pepper mixture.

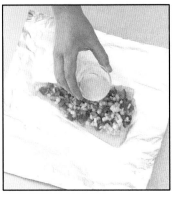

Drizzle with lemon juice and remaining oil. Season with salt and pepper then fold foil to make four parcels. Put parcels on a baking sheet and cook in oven 20 to 30 minutes or until fish flakes easily when tested with a knife. Unwrap foil parcels and transfer fish, vegetables and cooking juices to warmed serving plates. Garnish with lemon slices and serve.

Makes 4 servings.

— CHAR-BROILED TUNA SALAD —

12 oz. waxy new potatoes, scraped
4 oz. green beans, halved
4 tuna steaks, each weighing 6 oz.
1 little gem lettuce
Handful of rocket leaves
8 oz. cherry tomatoes, halved
8 hard-cooked quails' eggs, halved
1 (2-oz.) can anchovies in olive oil, drained
12 black olives
VINAIGRETTE:
1/2 teaspoon Dijon mustard
1 tablespoon white wine vinegar
Salt and freshly ground pepper
1/2 cup extra-virgin olive oil
1 tablespoon chopped fresh chives

To make vinaigrette, whisk together mustard, vinegar, salt and pepper. Whisk in olive oil then stir in chives. Set aside. Cook potatoes in boiling salted water 15 minutes, or until tender. Drain, slice and return to pan. Add 1 tablespoon of vinaigrette to potatoes, mix gently and let cool. Cook beans in boiling salted water 3 or 4 minutes or until tender but still crisp. Drain, rinse under cold water and drain again. Add beans to potatoes and mix together.

Brush tuna steaks on both sides with vinaigrette. Heat a ridged broiler pan or grill and cook tuna steaks 2 or 3 minutes on each side until browned but still slightly pink in center. Meanwhile, arrange lettuce leaves and rocket on serving plates. Drizzle with a little vinaigrette. Arrange potatoes, beans, tomatoes, eggs, anchovies and olives on top. Put tuna steaks on top of each salad, add remaining vinaigrette and serve.

Makes 4 servings.

—— HERB-CRUSTED SALMON ——

3 oz. olive ciabatta, crusts removed
4 anchovies in olive oil, drained and roughly chopped
1 shallot, roughly chopped
1 garlic clove, chopped
1 tablespoon chopped fresh basil
1 tablespoon chopped fresh parsley
Salt and freshly ground pepper
4 salmon steaks, each weighing 6 oz.
2 tablespoons olive oil
Basil sprigs, to garnish
SALSA ROSSA:
8 oz. cooked, peeled beetroot, diced
1 small red onion, finely chopped
1 teaspoon lemon juice
2 tablespoons olive oil
1 tablespoon chopped fresh parsley

Preheat oven to 400F (200C). To make salsa rossa, put beetroot in a bowl. Add onion. Season with salt and pepper and stir in lemon juice, olive oil and parsley. Set aside. Break ciabatta into pieces and put in a food processor. Add anchovies, shallot, garlic, basil, parsley, salt and pepper. Process until mixture forms coarse crumbs.

Press crumbs on top of salmon steaks and put steaks in an oiled ovenproof dish. Drizzle with olive oil. Cook in oven 15 minutes or until flesh flakes easily when tested with a knife. Garnish with basil sprigs and serve salmon with salsa rossa.

Makes 4 servings.

— SQUID IN TOMATO SAUCE —

1-1/2 lbs. squid
2 tablespoons olive oil
1 onion, chopped
1 garlic clove, chopped
1 (14-oz.) can crushed tomatoes
1/2 cup dry white wine
1 tablespoon tomato paste
2 teaspoons fresh oregano, chopped
Salt and freshly ground pepper
GREMOLATA:
2 tablespoons chopped fresh parsley
Grated zest of 1 lemon
1 garlic clove, finely chopped

To make gremolata, mix together parsley, lemon zest and garlic. Set aside.

To clean squid, pull head and tentacles away from body sac, bringing innards with it. Cut off tentacles and reserve. Remove ink sac. Pull transparent 'quill' from body. Rinse body and tentacles and dry well. Cut body into rings and cut tentacles in half.

Heat oil in a saucepan. Add onion and garlic and cook 5 minutes or until soft. Stir in tomatoes, wine, tomato paste, oregano, salt and pepper. Add squid and bring to a boil. Reduce heat, cover and simmer 30 to 40 minutes or until squid is tender. Sprinkle with gremolata and serve.

Makes 4 servings.

—— SEA BASS WITH FENNEL ——

1/4 cup olive oil
2 onions, thinly sliced
2 fennel bulbs, thinly sliced
1 fresh bay leaf
1 sea bass, about 2-3/4lbs., cleaned and scaled
Salt and freshly ground pepper
1 lemon, thinly sliced
1/3 cup dry white wine
Fennel leaves, to garnish

Preheat oven to 350F (180C). Heat 2 tablespoons of oil in a large skillet. Add onions and fennel and cook over low heat 3 minutes or until beginning to soften.

Transfer to a roasting pan. Put bay leaf inside fish and season with salt and pepper. Put fish on top of vegetables and cover it with lemon slices.

Add wine. Cover dish with foil and cook in oven 30 minutes or until fish flakes easily when tested with a knife. Remove lemon slices and drizzle remaining oil over fish. Cut fish into four fillets, garnish with fennel leaves and serve with vegetables and cooking juices.

Makes 4 servings.

STUFFED SARDINES

24 sardines, cleaned and heads removed
Juice of 1 lemon
Flour for dusting
Salt and freshly ground pepper
1/4 cup olive oil
STUFFING:
2 lbs. spinach
2 tablespoons olive oil
1 onion, chopped
2 garlic cloves, finely chopped
1/2 teaspoon freshly grated nutmeg
1 teaspoon chopped fresh thyme
1-1/2 cups fresh bread crumbs
1 egg, beaten
CUCUMBER AND MINT SALSA:
1/2 cucumber, seeded and diced
3 tablespoons chopped fresh mint
2 green onions, chopped
1 teaspoon white wine vinegar
2 tablespoons olive oil

Preheat oven to 450F (230C). To make stuffing, wash spinach and put in a saucepan. Cover and cook 5 minutes or until tender. Squeeze spinach dry and chop finely. Heat oil in a saucepan. Add onion and garlic and cook 5 minutes or until soft. Add spinach, nutmeg and thyme and cook 5 minutes. Let cool. Stir in bread crumbs and egg. Flatten sardines and remove backbones.

Sprinkle sardines with lemon juice. Dust skin with flour, salt and pepper. Spread twelve sardines with stuffing and put remaining sardines on top. Brush with oil, put in a roasting pan and cook in oven 10 minutes or until browned and tender. To make salsa, mix together cucumber, mint, green onions, vinegar, oil, salt and pepper. Serve with sardines.

Makes 4 servings.

— GREEK SEAFOOD CASSEROLE —

1 tablespoon olive oil
1 onion, chopped
1 garlic clove, crushed
1 stalk celery, chopped
Grated zest and juice of 1/2 lemon
4 large ripe tomatoes, peeled (page 17) and chopped
2 tablespoons chopped fresh parsley
1 fresh bay leaf
1 teaspoon dried oregano
Salt and freshly ground pepper
12 oz. monkfish fillet, skinned and cubed
8 oz. cleaned squid, cut into rings
1 lb. mussels, cleaned (page 56)
Chopped green olives, to garnish

Heat olive oil in a Dutch oven. Add onion, garlic and celery and cook 5 minutes or until soft. Add lemon zest and juice, tomatoes, parsley, bay leaf, oregano, salt and pepper. Bring to a boil, reduce heat, cover and simmer 20 minutes. Add monkfish to pan, adding a little water if necessary. Return to a boil, cover and cook 3 minutes.

Stir in squid and place mussels on top. Return to a boil, reduce heat, cover tightly and cook 5 minutes or until fish is tender and mussels have opened. Discard any mussels that remain closed. Garnish with chopped olives and serve.

Makes 4 servings.

——— SEARED SCALLOP SALAD ———

2 oz. sun-dried tomatoes
1 small bunch fresh basil
1/2 cup extra-virgin olive oil
2 tablespoons balsamic vinegar
Salt and freshly ground pepper
Mixed salad greens
1-1/2 lbs. shelled scallops
Basil sprigs, to garnish

Roughly chop sun-dried tomatoes. Remove basil leaves from stalks and roughly chop leaves.

Whisk together all but 1 tablespoon of olive oil, balsamic vinegar, salt and pepper. Stir in tomatoes and basil. Set aside. Put salad greens in a serving bowl. Heat a large heavy skillet until hot. Add remaining olive oil and wipe pan with paper towels to remove any excess.

Add scallops, in two batches if necessary, and cook 20 seconds. Turn and cook another 20 to 30 seconds until well browned. Return all scallops to pan. Remove from heat and add tomato mixture. Stir gently then pour immediately over salad greens. Garnish with basil and serve.

Makes 4 servings.

Note: If scallops are very large, cut them in half before cooking.

——— DEEP-FRIED MUSSELS ———

2-1/4lbs. mussels, cleaned (page 56)
Oil for deep-frying
BATTER:
1 cup all-purpose flour
2 tablespoons olive oil
1 egg white
BELL PEPPER SALSA:
1 red and 1 yellow bell pepper, roughly chopped
3 tablespoons olive oil
2 garlic cloves
1 tablespoon red wine vinegar
8 sun-dried tomatoes
1 small red onion, chopped
Salt and freshly ground pepper
2 tablespoons chopped fresh parsley

To make batter, sift flour and a pinch of salt into a bowl. Add oil and 3/4 cup water, beating to form a smooth cream. Let stand 1 hour. Put 3 tablespoons of water in a large saucepan and add mussels. Cover tightly and cook 3 to 5 minutes or until mussels have opened. Discard any that remain closed. Let cool then remove from shells.

To make salsa, put bell peppers in a food processor or blender with oil, garlic, vinegar, sun-dried tomatoes and onion. Blend until finely chopped. Season and add parsley. Whisk egg white until stiff and fold into batter. Heat oil in a large saucepan. Dip mussels into batter and cook, in batches, 3 or 4 minutes, or until golden. Drain on paper towels. Serve with bell pepper salsa.

Makes 4 servings.

— RED MULLET IN VINE LEAVES —

Juice of 1/2 lemon
1/4 cup olive oil
4 red mullet, cleaned and scaled
4 sprigs of fennel
8 vacuum-packed vine leaves, rinsed and dried
Lemon twists, to garnish
ROMESCO SAUCE:
1 large red bell pepper, peeled (page 28)
2 large ripe tomatoes, peeled (page 17)
Scant 1/2 cup olive oil
4 garlic cloves, chopped
1 fresh red chile, cored, seeded and chopped
1 slice day-old bread
1/4 cup ground almonds
2 tablespoons red wine vinegar
Salt and freshly ground pepper

To make romesco sauce, chop bell pepper and tomatoes. Heat 3 tablespoons of oil in a skillet. Add bell pepper, tomatoes, garlic and chile and cook over low heat 5 minutes. Break up bread and add to pan, turning in oil until lightly browned. Put mixture in a food processor or blender and process a few seconds. Add almonds, vinegar, salt and pepper. Process to a rough puree. With motor running, pour in remaining oil to form a thick sauce.

Preheat broiler. Mix together lemon juice and olive oil in a shallow dish. Add fish and turn in oil and lemon mixture. Put a fennel sprig inside each fish. Put two vine leaves side by side on work surface. Put a fish on top and roll up, pressing leaves together to seal. Brush with oil and lemon mixture. Broil 5 to 8 minutes on each side, until vine leaves are crisp and fish flakes easily. Garnish with lemon twists and serve with romesco sauce.

Makes 4 servings.

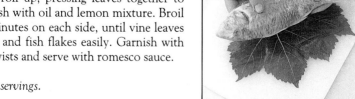

MARINATED FISH NIÇOISE

1 lb. sea bass, skinned and filleted
1 lb. salmon, skinned and filleted
8 scallops
Juice of 2 lemons
1 teaspoon sea salt
1 cup olive oil
1 teaspoon black peppercorns, lightly crushed
1 teaspoon coriander seeds, lightly crushed
1 tablespoon chopped fresh marjoram
3 fresh bay leaves
Lemon wedges and chopped fresh mint and parsley,
   to garnish

With a sharp knife, slice fish fillets as thinly as possible.

Cut scallops in half. Put fish and scallops in a shallow dish. Mix together lemon juice and salt until salt has dissolved. Whisk in half olive oil and add peppercorns, coriander seeds and marjoram. Pour over fish. Coarsely tear bay leaves and arrange amongst fish.

Cover dish and leave in a cool place 1 or 2 hours or until fish is opaque. Remove fish and scallops with a slotted spoon. Arrange on serving plates. Drizzle remaining oil over fish, garnish with lemon, mint and parsley and serve.

Makes 4 servings.

Note: It is lemon juice that 'cooks' fish in this recipe so it is important that fish is as fresh as possible. It is easier to slice thinly if it is thoroughly refrigerated.

MONKFISH KEBABS

1 small red onion, finely chopped
1 garlic clove, crushed
2 tablespoons chopped fresh cilantro
1/4 cup chopped fresh parsley
1 teaspoon ground cumin
1 teaspoon paprika
1/4 teaspoon chile powder
Pinch of saffron strands
1/4 cup olive oil
Juice of 1 lemon
1/2 teaspoon salt
1-1/2 lbs. monkfish fillets, skinned
Flat-leaf parsley sprigs and chives, to garnish
CHERRY TOMATO SALSA:
8 oz. red and yellow cherry tomatoes
1 small red onion, thinly sliced
1 quantity vinaigrette (page 43)
1 small fresh green chile, cored, seeded and sliced
1 tablespoon chopped fresh chives

Mix together onion, garlic, cilantro, parsley, cumin, paprika, chile powder, saffron, olive oil, lemon juice and salt. Cut monkfish into cubes and add to marinade. Mix well and leave in a cool place 1 hour

Meanwhile, make cherry tomato salsa. Halve tomatoes and put in a bowl. Add onion, vinaigrette, chile and chives. Mix well and let stand 30 minutes. Preheat broiler. Thread monkfish on to four skewers and put over broiler pan. Spoon a little of marinade over. Broil monkfish, close to heat, 3 minutes on each side until cooked through and lightly browned. Garnish with parsley sprigs and chives and serve with cherry tomato salsa.

Makes 4 servings.

GREY MULLET TAGINE

3/4 cup raisins
4 grey mullet fillets
2 tablespoons olive oil
1 onion, finely chopped
1/4 teaspoon coarsely crushed black peppercorns
1/4 teaspoon ground cinnamon
1/4 cup white wine vinegar
1/4 cup honey
Salt
2 tablespoons chopped fresh parsley
Flat-leaf parsley sprigs and lemon slices, to garnish
MARINADE:
1/4 cup olive oil
1/2 teaspoon ground cinnamon
1/4 teaspoon chile powder
1/2 teaspoon mixed spice

Put raisins in a bowl and cover with boiling water. Set aside. Put grey mullet in a shallow dish. To make marinade, mix together olive oil, 2 tablespoons water, cinnamon, chile powder and mixed spice. Pour over fish and leave in a cool place 2 hours. Heat olive oil in a skillet. Add onion and cook 5 minutes or until soft. Stir in peppercorns, cinnamon, vinegar, honey and salt. Drain raisins and add to pan.

Remove fish from marinade with a slotted spoon and set aside. Add marinade to pan. Bring to a boil, reduce heat and simmer 15 minutes. Add fish, spoon sauce over and simmer 10 minutes or until flesh flakes easily when tested with a knife. Garnish with parsley sprigs and lemon slices and serve.

Makes 4 servings.

CHAR-BROILED SCALLOPS

16 shelled scallops
Olive oil for brushing
Salt and freshly ground pepper
Lemon wedges and rocket leaves, to garnish
ROCKET PESTO:
2 oz. rocket
1 oz. pine nuts
2 garlic cloves, crushed
1/2 cup grated Parmesan cheese
Juice of 1/2 lemon
2/3 cup olive oil

To make rocket pesto, put rocket, pine nuts, garlic, Parmesan cheese and lemon juice in a food processor or blender.

Process until well blended. With motor running, gradually pour in olive oil until well combined. Season with salt and pepper. Transfer to a serving bowl and set aside. Cut each scallop in half. Thread scallops on to eight pairs of skewers.

Preheat a ridged broiler pan or grill. Brush scallops with olive oil and season with salt. Put skewers on broiler pan and broil 1 minute. Turn and broil another minute until browned on outside but still moist in center. Garnish with lemon wedges and rocket leaves and serve with rocket pesto.

Makes 4 servings.

Note: Double skewers are best for holding scallops in place.

BAKED ALMOND MUSSELS

2-1/4 lbs. mussels
1/2 cup olive oil
2 shallots, chopped
2/3 cup dry white wine
1/2 cup bread crumbs
1/4 cup ground almonds
2 tablespoons chopped fresh parsley
1 garlic clove, finely chopped
Salt and freshly ground pepper
Flaked almonds and flat-leaf parsley sprigs, to
   garnish

Scrub mussels, scrape off any barnacles and remove any beards. Discard any that do not close when tapped.

Preheat oven to 450F (230C). Heat 2 tablespoons of oil in a large saucepan. Add shallots and cook 3 minutes or until soft. Add mussels and wine. Bring to a boil, reduce heat, cover tightly and cook 5 minutes or until mussels have opened. Remove mussels with a slotted spoon, discarding any that remain closed. Strain cooking liquid through a strainer lined with paper towels. Remove top shell from each mussel and arrange lower shells on two baking sheets.

Mix together bread crumbs, ground almonds, parsley, garlic, salt and pepper. Add remaining oil and 2 tablespoons of strained cooking liquid. Put a little bread crumb mixture on top of each mussel, pressing it down to fill shell. Cook in oven 7 to 10 minutes or until topping is golden, being careful not to overcook it. Garnish with flaked almonds and flat-leaf parsley and serve.

Makes 4 servings.

LE GRAND AÏOLI

2-1/4lbs. salt cod
2 sprigs of thyme
2 fresh bay leaves
1 onion
2/3 cup dry white wine
12 hard-cooked quails' eggs
3 fennel bulbs, cooked
3 baby globe artichokes, cooked
12 small potatoes, cooked
8oz. green beans, cooked
3 baby red or green bell peppers
12 black olives, to garnish
AÏOLI:
1-1/2 cups mayonnaise
4 garlic cloves, crushed

Put salt cod in a large bowl and cover with plenty of cold water. Leave to soak at least 12 hours, changing water frequently. Drain, remove skin and bones and break fish into chunks. Put in a saucepan with thyme, bay leaves, onion and wine. Cover with cold water. Bring to a boil, reduce heat and simmer 12 to 15 minutes or until fish is just tender. Drain well, discarding herbs and onion. Rinse under cold water and drain again. Coarsely shred fish.

To make aïoli, mix together mayonnaise and garlic. Arrange fish in center of four serving plates. Cut quails' eggs lengthwise in half. Halve or quarter fennel and artichokes. Arrange eggs, fennel, artichokes, potatoes and beans around cod. Cut bell peppers in half and remove core and seeds. Divide aïoli among bell pepper cups and serve with fish and vegetables, garnished with olives.

Makes 6 servings.

— SHRIMP WITH MAYONNAISE —

3 tablespoons olive oil
Juice of 1/2 lemon
2 garlic cloves, crushed
1 tablespoon chopped fresh fennel
Salt and freshly ground pepper
20 raw jumbo shrimp
Radicchio leaves and fennel sprigs, to garnish
SAFFRON MAYONNAISE:
2/3 cup fish stock
Generous pinch of saffron strands
2/3 cup mayonnaise
1 teaspoon lemon juice

Mix together oil, lemon juice, garlic, fennel, salt and pepper.

Put shrimp in a shallow dish and pour marinade over. Turn to coat in marinade. Leave in a cool place 2 hours. To make saffron mayonnaise, put fish stock in a saucepan and boil until reduced to 1 tablespoon. Add saffron strands and let cool. Strain stock into a bowl and stir in mayonnaise. Add lemon juice, salt and pepper.

Preheat broiler. Remove shrimp from marinade and thread on to skewers. Broil 10 minutes, turning once. Remove from skewers and arrange on serving plates. Garnish with radicchio leaves and fennel and serve with saffron mayonnaise.

Makes 4 servings.

SEAFOOD PAELLA

3 tablespoons olive oil
9 oz. monkfish fillet, skinned and cubed
1 Spanish onion, chopped
2 garlic cloves, finely chopped
1 green bell pepper, diced
1-1/3 cups Arborio rice
3 cups fish stock
2/3 cup dry white wine
3 ripe tomatoes, peeled (page 17) and chopped
1 teaspoon saffron strands
14 oz. mixed cooked shellfish
4 oz. fresh shelled peas
Salt and freshly ground pepper

Heat olive oil in a large skillet. Add monkfish and cook 5 minutes.

Remove with a slotted spoon and set aside. Add onion and garlic to pan and cook 5 minutes or until soft. Add bell pepper and cook 2 minutes. Add rice and stir to coat with oil. Pour in stock and wine and add tomatoes and saffron. Bring to a boil, reduce heat and simmer, uncovered, 20 minutes.

Add monkfish and cook 5 to 10 minutes or until most of stock has been absorbed and rice is tender. Reserve some shellfish for garnish and add remainder to pan with peas. Cook 5 minutes or until heated through. Add a little more stock if necessary. Season with salt and pepper, garnish with reserved shellfish and serve.

Makes 4 servings.

Note: Ready-prepared mixed shellfish is available from many supermarkets.

CHICKEN PUTTANESCA

1/4 cup olive oil
1 red onion
2 garlic cloves, crushed
1 (2-oz.) can anchovies in olive oil, drained
1 oz. black olives, pitted
1 oz. sun-dried tomatoes
1 (14-oz.) can crushed tomatoes
1/2 teaspoon crushed dried chiles
2 teaspoons chopped fresh oregano
1 tablespoon balsamic vinegar
Salt and freshly ground pepper
8 skinless, boneless chicken thighs
Oregano sprigs, to garnish

Heat half oil in a large saucepan. Add onion and garlic and cook 5 minutes.

Chop anchovies, olives and sun-dried tomatoes. Add to pan with tomatoes, chiles, oregano, balsamic vinegar, salt and pepper. Bring to a boil. Heat remaining oil in a large skillet. Add chicken and cook until browned all over.

Remove with a slotted spoon and add to saucepan. Turn to coat with sauce. Cover and simmer 30 minutes or until chicken is cooked through. Garnish with oregano and serve.

Makes 4 servings.

—— BOURRIDE OF CHICKEN ——

2 tablespoons olive oil
1 (3-lb.) chicken, cut into 8 pieces
4 shallots, chopped
1 leek, chopped
2/3 cup dry white wine
1/2 teaspoon saffron strands
Cooked baby leeks, to serve
GARLIC SAUCE:
8 garlic cloves
2/3 cup mayonnaise

Heat olive oil in a Dutch oven. Add chicken pieces and cook until browned all over. Remove with a slotted spoon and set aside.

Add shallots and leek to pan and cook 3 minutes or until soft. Return chicken to pan and add wine and saffron. Bring to a boil, reduce heat, cover and simmer 30 to 40 minutes or until chicken is cooked through. Meanwhile, make garlic sauce. Put unpeeled garlic cloves in a small saucepan and add enough water to cover. Bring to a boil, reduce heat and simmer 15 minutes or until soft. Drain and let cool.

Put mayonnaise in a food processor or blender. Squeeze softened garlic out of skin into food processor or blender. Remove chicken from pan and place on a warmed serving dish. Add cooking juices to food processor or blender and quickly process. Pour over chicken. Serve with baby leeks.

Makes 4 servings.

GREEK CHICKEN PIES

1 (3-lb.) chicken
Chicken stock
1 lb. onions, roughly chopped
2/3 cup milk
Grated zest of 1/2 lemon
2 teaspoons lemon juice
2 oz. feta cheese
1/4 teaspoon grated nutmeg
1 tablespoon chopped fresh parsley
1 egg, beaten
Salt and freshly ground pepper
12 sheets filo pastry, about 16- x 12-inch
1/4 cup butter, melted

Put chicken in a Dutch oven into which it fits tightly.

Pour in enough stock to almost cover legs. Cover breast with buttered parchment paper. Bring to a boil, reduce heat, cover and simmer 1 hour or until tender. Remove from pan and let cool. Add onions and milk to pan. Boil rapidly until liquid is reduced to 1-1/4 cups. Preheat oven to 350F (180C). Remove skin from chicken. Cut meat into bite-size pieces and put in a large bowl. Stir in onion and milk mixture, lemon zest and juice, feta cheese, nutmeg, parsley, egg, salt and pepper.

Cut each sheet of pastry crosswise in half. Lightly brush one sheet of pastry with melted butter and place in a 4-inch tartlet pan. Lightly butter three more sheets and layer on top, letting pastry overhang edge. Repeat with five more tartlet pans. Add chicken mixture to pans. Fold overhanging pastry over top. Brush with butter. Cook in oven 30 minutes or until golden and crisp. Serve at once.

Makes 6 servings.

— MOROCCAN ROAST CHICKEN —

2 tablespoons butter
1 onion, chopped
1 garlic clove, crushed
1-1/2 teaspoons ground cinnamon
1/2 teaspoon ground cumin
1 oz. blanched almonds, finely chopped
1-1/2 cups mixed dried fruit, soaked and chopped
Salt and freshly ground pepper
1 (3-1/2-lb.) chicken
2 teaspoons paprika
2 tablespoons olive oil
2 teaspoons honey
1/4 cup lemon juice
1 tablespoon tomato paste
2/3 cup chicken stock
1/2 to 1 teaspoon harissa

Melt butter in a saucepan. Add onion and garlic and cook over low heat 5 minutes or until soft. Add cinnamon and cumin and cook, stirring, 2 minutes. Add almonds and fruit, season with salt and pepper and cook 2 minutes. Let cool. Preheat oven to 400F (200C). Stuff neck end of chicken with fruit mixture. Set aside any excess. Mix together paprika and oil and brush over chicken. Put chicken in a roasting pan and roast 1 to 1-1/4 hours, basting occasionally, until chicken is cooked.

Transfer chicken to a carving board. Pour any excess fat from roasting pan. Stir honey, lemon juice, tomato paste, stock and harissa into juices in roasting pan. Add salt to taste. Bring to a boil, reduce heat and simmer 2 minutes. Reheat any excess stuffing. Carve chicken and serve with stuffing and sauce.

Makes 4 or 5 servings.

MOZZARELLA CHICKEN

4 skinless, boneless chicken breasts
2 teaspoons pesto
3 oz. smoked mozzarella cheese, thinly sliced
4 slices prosciutto
2 tablespoons butter
3 oz. shallots, very finely chopped
2/3 cup dry white wine
1 teaspoon Dijon mustard
Salt and freshly ground pepper
Basil sprigs, to garnish

Cut a horizontal slit along each chicken breast to form a pocket. Spread a little pesto in each pocket.

Put mozzarella slices into pockets. Wrap a slice of prosciutto around each chicken breast. Tie with fine string or cotton. Melt butter in a skillet, add shallots and cook over low heat 3 minutes or until soft. Add chicken breasts and cook until lightly browned on each side. Pour in wine. Bring to a boil, reduce heat, cover and simmer 20 minutes or until chicken is cooked through and tender.

Remove chicken with a slotted spoon and keep warm. Stir mustard into pan. Season with salt and pepper and allow to bubble 1 minute. Remove string or cotton from chicken. With a sharp knife, slice each breast and arrange on warmed serving plates. Pour sauce over chicken, garnish with basil sprigs and serve.

Makes 4 servings.

Note: Use plain mozzarella if smoked variety is unavailable.

BASQUE CHICKEN

1-1/4 cups hot chicken stock
1/2 teaspoon saffron strands
3 tablespoons olive oil
1 (3-3/4-lb.) chicken, cut into 8 pieces
1 onion, chopped
1 garlic clove, finely chopped
1 red bell pepper, cut into strips
1-1/2 cups long grain rice
1 (14-oz.) can crushed tomatoes
1 teaspoon paprika
8 oz. chorizo sausage, sliced
Salt and freshly ground pepper
1-1/4 cups dry white wine
Basil sprigs and orange slices, to garnish

Put stock in a measuring cup and add saffron.

Let stand. Heat oil in a large, deep skillet. Add chicken pieces and cook until browned all over. Remove with a slotted spoon and keep warm. Add onion, garlic and bell pepper to pan and cook until soft. Stir in rice. Add tomatoes and bring to a boil.

Add paprika, chorizo, salt and pepper and cook, stirring, 2 minutes. Strain stock, discarding saffron strands. Add wine and strained stock to pan. Return chicken to pan, bring to a boil, reduce heat, cover and simmer 45 minutes or until chicken and rice are cooked and liquid has been absorbed. Garnish with basil sprigs and orange slices and serve.

Makes 4 servings.

— CHICKEN BULGHUR PILAFF —

4 skinless, boneless chicken breasts, cubed
Juice of 1/2 lemon
1 tablespoon olive oil
1 onion, finely chopped
2 tablespoons pine nuts
2 tablespoons dried currants
1 teaspoon ground cumin
1-1/4 cups bulghur wheat
2-1/2 cups hot chicken stock
Salt and freshly ground pepper
Chopped fresh parsley, to garnish

Put chicken in a bowl and stir in lemon juice.

Heat olive oil in a large, deep skillet. Add onion and pine nuts and cook over low heat 7 minutes or until onion is soft and beginning to colour. Add chicken and cook, stirring, 8 to 10 minutes. Stir in currants and cumin then add bulghur wheat and cook, stirring, 2 minutes.

Add half hot stock and season with salt and pepper. Bring to a boil, reduce heat, cover and simmer until stock has been absorbed. Add remaining stock, cover and cook until bulghur wheat is tender and stock has been absorbed. Garnish with chopped parsley and serve.

Makes 4 servings.

—— TURKEY PARMIGIANA ——

1/4 cup olive oil
1 onion, chopped
1 garlic clove, crushed
1 (14-oz.) can crushed tomatoes
1 teaspoon dried oregano
Salt and freshly ground pepper
9 oz. eggplant, thinly sliced
4 turkey steaks
4 oz. mozzarella cheese, thinly sliced
1/4 cup grated Parmesan cheese

Heat 1 tablespoon of olive oil in a saucepan. Add onion and garlic and cook 5 minutes or until soft. Add tomatoes, oregano, salt and pepper.

Bring to a boil, reduce heat and simmer 2 minutes. Pour into a shallow ovenproof dish and set aside. Preheat oven to 375F (190C). Preheat broiler. Brush eggplant with 2 tablespoons of oil. Broil a few minutes on each side until soft and lightly browned. Set aside.

Heat remaining oil in a skillet, add turkey steaks and cook 2 or 3 minutes on each side until browned. Put turkey steaks on top of tomato sauce. Arrange eggplant and mozzarella slices on top, overlapping. Sprinkle with Parmesan cheese and cook in oven 30 minutes or until turkey is cooked through and topping is browned.

Makes 4 servings.

— PHEASANT WITH SULTANAS —

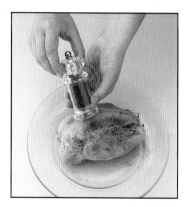

1/3 cup sultanas
1/2 cup medium sherry
1/4 cup olive oil
1 young pheasant
Salt and freshly ground pepper
1 oz. pine nuts

Preheat oven to 375F (190C). Put sultanas in a small bowl, add sherry and leave to soak. Rub 2 tablespoons of oil over pheasant and season with salt and pepper.

Put pheasant in a roasting pan and roast 30 to 45 minutes or until cooked through and tender. Just before pheasant is ready, drain sultanas, reserving sherry. Heat remaining oil in a skillet and cook pine nuts until golden. Add sultanas and cook 1 minute.

Carve pheasant and arrange on warmed serving plates. Scatter with pine nuts and sultanas and keep warm. Pour reserved sherry into roasting pan and heat, stirring to incorporate any sediment. Pour over pheasant and serve.

Makes 2 or 3 servings.

– QUAIL WITH FIGS & ORANGES –

3 tablespoons olive oil
8 quails
1 onion, thinly sliced
2 stalks celery, thinly sliced
2/3 cup dry white wine
2/3 cup hot chicken stock
Salt and freshly ground pepper
2 oranges
4 figs

Preheat oven to 325F (160C). Heat 2 tablespoons olive oil in a heavy pan. Add quails and cook until browned all over. Remove and set aside.

Add onion and celery to pan and cook over low heat 7 minutes or until soft and lightly browned. Replace quails and add wine and hot stock. Season with salt and pepper. Cover and cook in oven 30 to 40 minutes or until quails are cooked through. Just before end of cooking time, preheat broiler. Peel oranges, removing all pith and cut each one into four thick slices. Cut figs in half.

Brush orange slices with olive oil and broil 2 or 3 minutes. Turn, add figs and broil cut sides 2 minutes. Set aside and keep warm. Transfer quails, onion and celery to a warmed serving dish. Add cooking juices, arrange oranges and figs around birds and serve.

Makes 4 servings.

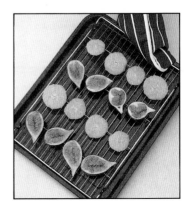

MEDITERRANEAN DUCK

1 tablespoon olive oil
1 (4-lb.) duck, quartered
1 large onion, thinly sliced
1 garlic clove, crushed
1/2 teaspoon ground cumin
1-3/4 cups chicken stock
Juice of 1/2 lemon
1 or 2 teaspoons harissa
1 cinnamon stick
1 teaspoon saffron strands
2 oz. black olives
2 oz. green olives
Zest of 1 preserved lemon, rinsed and cut into strips
Salt and freshly ground pepper
2 tablespoons chopped fresh cilantro
Cilantro sprigs, to garnish

Heat oil in a Dutch oven. Add duck and cook until browned all over. Remove with a slotted spoon and set aside. Add onion and garlic to pan and cook 5 minutes or until soft. Add cumin and cook, stirring, 2 minutes.

Add stock, lemon juice, harissa, cinnamon and saffron. Bring to a boil. Return duck to pan and add olives and lemon zest. Season with salt and pepper. Simmer, partially covered, 45 minutes or until duck is cooked through. Discard cinnamon stick. Stir in chopped cilantro, garnish and serve.

Makes 4 servings.

Note: If preserved lemons are unavailable, use grated zest of 1 fresh lemon instead.

PIGEONS STIFADO

4 pigeons
2 tablespoons seasoned flour
1/3 cup olive oil
1 lb. tiny pickling onions, peeled
1 garlic clove, crushed
1 tablespoon tomato paste
3/4 cup red wine
1 cup chicken stock
1 fresh bay leaf
2 sprigs of thyme
Salt and freshly ground pepper
2 slices white bread, crusts removed
2 tablespoons chopped fresh parsley

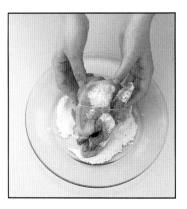

Toss pigeons in seasoned flour. Preheat oven to 325F (160C).

Heat half oil in a Dutch oven. Add pigeons and cook until browned all over. Remove and set aside. Add onions to pan and cook 7 minutes or until beginning to brown. Add garlic and tomato paste and stir in wine and stock. Add bay leaf, thyme, salt and pepper. Return pigeons to pan, cover and cook in oven 1-1/2 to 2 hours or until pigeons are cooked through and tender. Transfer pigeons to a warmed serving dish and keep warm.

Remove herbs from cooking liquid and, if liked, reduce cooking liquid by boiling over high heat 1 or 2 minutes. Cut each slice of bread into four triangles. Heat remaining oil in a skillet, add bread and fry until golden brown on both sides. Dip one edge of each triangle into parsley. Pour sauce over pigeons, garnish with fried bread and serve.

Makes 4 servings.

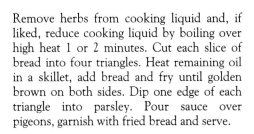

PROVENÇAL RABBIT

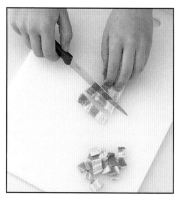

3 oz. pancetta
2 tablespoons olive oil
1 onion, chopped
4 rabbit portions
1 tablespoon seasoned flour
3 tablespoons tapénade (see below)
1-3/4 cups chicken stock
2/3 cup dry white wine
2 fresh bay leaves
2 sprigs of thyme
Salt and freshly ground pepper
1 small fennel bulb, roughly chopped
Black olives and fennel leaves, to garnish

Preheat oven to 350F (180C). Roughly chop half pancetta.

Heat half oil in a Dutch oven. Add onion and chopped pancetta and cook 3 minutes. Remove with a slotted spoon and set aside. Dust rabbit portions with seasoned flour. Heat remaining oil in pan, add rabbit and cook until browned all over. Mix together tapénade, stock and wine and pour over rabbit. Add onion, pancetta, bay leaves and thyme. Season with salt and pepper and bring to a boil. Cover and cook in oven 45 minutes.

Add fennel and cook 45 minutes or until rabbit is cooked through and tender. Broil remaining pancetta until crisp then snip into small pieces. Scatter pancetta over rabbit. Garnish with olives and fennel leaves and serve.

Makes 4 servings.

Note: If you don't have time to make your own tapénade (page 21), it can be bought ready made, in small jars.

— ROAST LAMB & VEGETABLES —

1 garlic clove, crushed
1 teaspoon chopped fresh mint
1 teaspoon chopped fresh rosemary
1 teaspoon chopped fresh oregano
Salt and freshly ground pepper
1 square-cut lamb shoulder weighing about 4lb, boned
1-1/2lbs. potatoes, thinly sliced
1 large onion, thinly sliced
1lb. tomatoes, sliced
1/2 cup dry white wine
Mint, rosemary and oregano sprigs, to garnish

Preheat oven to 425F (220C). Mix together garlic, mint, rosemary, oregano, salt and pepper.

Spread herb mixture over inside of lamb then roll up and tie into a neat shape. Put in a large roasting pan. Reduce oven temperature to 350F (180C) and roast lamb 30 minutes. Spoon any fat from roasting pan and add potatoes, onion and tomatoes.

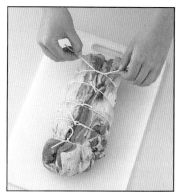

Add wine and season with salt and pepper. Cook 1 hour, turning vegetables occasionally. Carve lamb and arrange on warmed serving plates with vegetables. Add cooking juices. Garnish with mint, rosemary and oregano sprigs and serve.

Makes 6 servings.

TUNISIAN LAMB BURGERS

1 lb. ground lamb
1 small onion, finely chopped
1 garlic clove, crushed
1/2 teaspoon each ground cumin and coriander
1/2 to 1 teaspoon harissa
2 teaspoons each chopped fresh oregano and parsley
Olive oil for brushing
TOMATO SALSA:
2 large tomatoes, peeled (page 17) and seeded
1/4 cucumber, peeled, quartered and seeded
1 small red onion
1 garlic clove, crushed
Salt and freshly ground pepper
Grated zest of 1/2 lemon

To make tomato salsa, roughly chop tomatoes, cucumber and onion. Put in a food processor or blender with garlic. Process until finely chopped. Season with salt and pepper and stir in lemon zest. Transfer to a serving bowl and refrigerate until required.

Mix together lamb, onion, garlic, cumin, coriander, harissa, oregano, parsley and salt until well combined. Form into four burgers. Heat a ridged broiler pan. Brush burgers lightly with olive oil and cook 3 minutes on each side medium rare or 5 minutes for well done. Serve with tomato salsa.

Makes 4 servings.

MOROCCAN LAMB

1 cup dried apricots
2 tablespoons olive oil
1 large onion, chopped
2-1/4lbs. boneless shoulder of lamb, cubed
1 teaspoon ground cumin
1/2 teaspoon each ground coriander and cinnamon
Salt and freshly ground pepper
Grated zest and juice of 1/2 orange
1 teaspoon saffron strands
1 tablespoon ground almonds
About 1-1/4 cups lamb or chicken stock
1 tablespoon sesame seeds
Flat-leaf parsley sprigs, to garnish

Cut apricots in half and put in a bowl.

Cover with 2/3 cup water and leave to soak overnight. Preheat oven to 350F (180C). Heat olive oil in a Dutch oven. Add onion and cook over low heat 10 minutes or until soft and golden. Add lamb, cumin, coriander, cinnamon, salt and pepper and cook, stirring, 5 minutes.

Add apricots and their soaking liquid. Stir in orange zest and juice, saffron, ground almonds and enough stock to cover. Cover and cook in oven 1 to 1-1/2 hours or until meat is tender, adding extra stock if necessary. Heat a skillet, add sesame seeds and dry fry, shaking pan, until golden. Sprinkle sesame seeds over meat, garnish with parsley and serve.

Makes 4 to 6 servings.

LAMB YOGURTLU

2 pitta breads
3 tablespoons olive oil
1 lb. boneless leg of lamb, cubed
12 oz. tomatoes, peeled and coarsely chopped
Salt and freshly ground pepper
1-1/4 cups regular plain yogurt, at room temperature
1 oz. pine nuts
2 tablespoons chopped fresh parsley

Split pitta breads in half and cut each half into four triangles. Heat half oil in a skillet. Add lamb and cook until browned all over.

Reduce heat and cook 10 minutes or until cooked through. Remove with a slotted spoon and keep warm. Toast pitta bread triangles and keep warm. Heat remaining oil in a skillet. Add tomatoes and cook briefly until just softened but still retaining their shape.

Reserve four pitta triangles and put remainder on warmed serving plates. Pour tomatoes and their juice over triangles and season with salt and pepper. Spoon most of yogurt over tomatoes. Arrange lamb on top and spoon remaining yogurt over. Sprinkle with pine nuts and chopped parsley, arrange reserved pitta triangles at side and serve.

Makes 4 servings.

SOUVLAKIA

2 garlic cloves, crushed
1/4 cup lemon juice
2 tablespoons olive oil
1/4 cup chopped fresh oregano
Salt and freshly ground pepper
1 lb. lean lamb fillet, cubed
6 fresh bay leaves, halved
Oregano sprigs, to garnish
TOMATO AND OLIVE SALSA:
6 oz. mixed green and black olives, pitted and finely
  chopped
1 small red onion, finely chopped
4 plum tomatoes, finely chopped
2 tablespoons olive oil

In a shallow dish, mix together garlic, lemon juice, olive oil, oregano, salt and pepper. Add lamb and mix well. Leave in a cool place 2 hours. To make salsa, put olives, onion, tomatoes, olive oil, salt and pepper in a bowl and mix together. Refrigerate until required.

Remove lamb from marinade and thread on to skewers, adding bay leaves to skewers at regular intervals. Broil over a grill or under a hot broiler, turning occasionally, 10 minutes or until lamb is brown and crisp on outside and pink and juicy inside. Garnish with oregano sprigs and serve with tomato and olive salsa.

Makes 4 servings.

SPICY BRAISED BEEF

2 garlic cloves, crushed
1/2 teaspoon ground cinnamon
1/4 teaspoon ground cloves
Salt and freshly ground pepper
1 (3-lb.) lean beef top round roast
3 tablespoons olive oil
4 onions, thinly sliced
1/2 cup red wine
2 tablespoons tomato paste
1 lb. spaghetti
1 tablespoon balsamic vinegar

Mix together garlic, cinnamon, cloves, salt and pepper. Make incisions in beef and push in garlic mixture.

Leave in a cool place 1 hour. Heat oil in a pan into which meat will just fit. Add meat and cook, turning, until browned all over. Remove from pan. Add onions and cook over low heat until soft and lightly browned. Replace meat, add wine and enough water to barely cover. Mix tomato paste with a little water. Stir into pan. Season, cover and simmer, turning meat frequently, about 1-1/2 hours or until tender.

Bring a large saucepan of salted water to a boil. Cook spaghetti according to package instructions until just tender. Drain. Remove meat from pan and keep warm. Add vinegar to sauce. Boil over high heat until reduced to a smooth glossy sauce. Slice beef and arrange on warmed serving plates. Pour a little sauce over beef, stir remainder into spaghetti and serve with beef.

Makes 6 servings.

—— PROVENÇAL BEEF DAUBE ——

1 large onion, chopped
1-1/4 cups red wine
3 garlic cloves, crushed
2 fresh bay leaves
1 sprig of thyme
Salt and freshly ground pepper
2-1/4 lbs. lean beef chuck, cubed
2 tablespoons olive oil
6 oz. bacon, diced
1 tablespoon all-purpose flour
2 tablespoons balsamic vinegar
2 ripe tomatoes, chopped
6-inch strip pared orange zest
12 black olives, pitted and halved
1-1/4 to 2-1/2 cups beef stock

Put onion, wine, garlic, bay leaves, thyme, salt and pepper in a large shallow dish and mix well. Add beef and stir well to coat. Cover and leave in a cool place overnight. Preheat oven to 325F (160C). Remove beef from marinade, reserving marinade, and pat beef dry on paper towels. Heat oil in a Dutch oven, add bacon and cook until golden. Remove with a slotted spoon and set aside.

Add beef to pan and cook until browned all over. Sprinkle on flour and cook 1 minute, stirring. Add reserved marinade and vinegar. Add tomatoes, orange zest and olives. Pour in enough stock to cover beef and season with salt and pepper. Cover tightly and cook in oven 3 hours or until beef is tender. If necessary, add more stock during cooking. Discard bay leaves, thyme and orange zest and serve.

Makes 4 to 6 servings.

—— STUFFED VEGETABLES ——

4 baby eggplant
4 zucchini
4 baby red bell peppers
4 tomatoes
2 slices white bread, crusts removed
3 tablespoons olive oil
1 onion, finely chopped
1 garlic clove, finely chopped
8oz. lean ground beef
2 tablespoons each chopped fresh cilantro and
    parsley
1/2 teaspoon each ground cumin, cinnamon and
    paprika
Salt and freshly ground pepper
1 egg, beaten
Cilantro sprigs, to garnish

Bring a saucepan of salted water to a boil. Add eggplant, zucchini and bell peppers and cook 3 minutes. Drain. Cut tops off eggplant, bell peppers and tomatoes. Cut a strip from one side of each zucchini. Hollow out eggplant, zucchini and tomatoes, leaving a shell about 1/4-inch thick. Roughly chop flesh. Remove core and seeds from bell peppers. Preheat oven to 350F (180C). Soak bread in cold water 10 minutes.

Heat 1 tablespoon of olive oil in a skillet. Add onion and garlic and cook 5 minutes or until soft. Add beef and cook until browned. Squeeze bread dry and crumble into pan with chopped vegetables, herbs, spices, salt and pepper. Cook 1 or 2 minutes. Transfer to a bowl. Allow to cool a little then mix in egg. Use to stuff vegetables. Drizzle with remaining oil and cook in oven 30 minutes. Garnish with cilantro sprigs and serve.

Makes 4 servings.

ZUCCHINI MOUSSAKA

3 tablespoons olive oil
3 zucchini, thinly sliced
1 large onion, finely chopped
1 garlic clove, crushed
1-1/2lbs. ground beef or lamb
1 (7-oz.) can crushed tomatoes
1 tablespoon tomato paste
2 teaspoons dried oregano
1 teaspoon ground cinnamon
1/2 cup red wine
1/2 cup beef or lamb stock
Salt and freshly ground pepper
12oz. cooked potato, thinly sliced
4 tomatoes, thinly sliced
SAUCE:
1/4 cup butter
1/2 cup all-purpose flour
2 cups milk
2/3 cup regular plain yogurt
1/4 cup grated Asiago cheese

Heat 2 tablespoons of oil in a large saucepan. Add zucchini and cook 3 minutes. Remove with a slotted spoon and drain on paper towels. Heat remaining oil in saucepan and cook onion and garlic until soft. Add beef and cook until browned. Add tomatoes, tomato paste, oregano, cinnamon, wine, stock, salt and pepper. Cover and simmer 30 minutes.

Uncover and cook until any liquid evaporates. Preheat oven to 350F (180C). To make sauce, melt butter in a saucepan, add flour and cook, stirring, 2 minutes. Remove from heat and stir in milk and yogurt. Cook, stirring, until thickened. Simmer 5 minutes. Season. Put meat in an ovenproof dish. Top with layers of potato, zucchini and tomato. Spoon sauce over and sprinkle with cheese. Cook in oven 40 minutes.

Makes 6 servings.

GREEK MEATBALLS

1 slice white bread, crusts removed
1 lb. ground veal
1 garlic clove, crushed
1 onion, finely chopped
1 tablespoon chopped fresh parsley
1 tablespoon chopped fresh mint
1/2 teaspoon ground cinnamon
Salt and freshly ground pepper
All-purpose flour for dusting
2 tablespoons olive oil
Flat-leaf parsley and mint sprigs, to garnish
Greek Yogurt Dip (page 22) and pitta bread, to
    serve

Soak bread in cold water 10 minutes. Squeeze dry and crumble into a bowl.

Add veal, garlic, onion, parsley, mint, cinnamon, salt and pepper and mix thoroughly. On a floured surface, roll meat mixture into small balls and dust lightly with flour.

Heat oil in a skillet and fry meatballs 5 or 6 minutes, turning frequently, until browned and cooked through. Remove with a slotted spoon and transfer to a warmed serving dish. Garnish with parsley and mint and serve with Greek Yogurt Dip and pitta bread.

Makes 6 servings.

AFELIA

2 teaspoons coriander seeds
1 teaspoon black peppercorns
2 teaspoons light brown sugar
4 pork chops
1 tablespoon olive oil
1-1/4 cups dry white wine
2 tablespoons butter, diced
Salt
2 teaspoons chopped fresh cilantro
Cilantro sprigs, to garnish

In a pestle and mortar, lightly crush coriander seeds and peppercorns. Stir in brown sugar. Rub mixture into both sides of chops.

Put chops in a shallow dish and leave in a cool place 1 to 4 hours. Heat oil in a large skillet. Add chops and cook until browned on both sides. Pour in wine and let it bubble 1 minute. Reduce heat and simmer 20 to 30 minutes, turning occasionally, until chops are cooked through.

Transfer chops to a warmed serving dish. If sauce is too thin, boil 1 or 2 minutes or until reduced and thickened to a syrupy sauce. Stir in butter, season with salt and stir in cilantro. Garnish with cilantro sprigs and serve.

Makes 4 servings.

PORK SALTIMBOCCA

4 slices pork fillet, about 3 or 4oz. each
4 slices prosciutto
4 sage leaves
2 tablespoons all-purpose flour
4 teaspoons olive oil
2/3 cup medium white wine
Freshly ground pepper
1 tablespoon butter, diced

Put pork fillet between 2 sheets of plastic wrap and beat out thinly. Lay a slice of prosciutto on each slice of pork, trimming prosciutto to fit if necessary.

Put a sage leaf on top and secure with a wooden cocktail stick. Dust each piece of meat with flour, shaking off any excess. Heat oil in a skillet. Add pork and cook 1 minute on each side. Remove from pan and keep warm.

Add wine to pan, stirring to incorporate any sediment. Replace pork and cook in wine 3 minutes or until tender. Remove pork with a slotted spoon and transfer to a warmed serving dish. Allow wine to bubble 1 minute, season with black pepper and stir in butter. Pour over pork and serve.

Makes 4 servings.

— GREEK PORK & PASTA BAKE —

4 thick pork steaks or chops
Salt and freshly ground pepper
2 garlic cloves, sliced
2-1/2 cups hot chicken stock
1 (14-oz.) can crushed tomatoes
3 tablespoons olive oil
1 tablespoon chopped fresh marjoram
1 tablespoon chopped fresh parsley
8 oz. orzo (rice-shaped pasta)

Preheat oven to 400F (200C). Season pork with salt and pepper. Put in a single layer in a large roasting pan.

Scatter garlic over pork. Add half stock, tomatoes and oil. Sprinkle with marjoram and parsley and season with salt and pepper. Cook 30 minutes, turning meat halfway through cooking.

Add remaining hot stock and pasta to roasting pan. Cook 30 to 40 minutes or until pasta is cooked and meat is tender. If necessary, add more hot stock or water during cooking. Serve.

Makes 4 servings.

PORK & CLAMS

2-1/4 lbs. loin of pork, cubed
3 tablespoons olive oil
1 onion, chopped
2 teaspoons tomato paste
Salt and freshly ground pepper
2-1/4 lbs. clams, cleaned
Cilantro leaves and lemon wedges, to garnish
MARINADE:
2 teaspoons balsamic vinegar
1-1/4 cups dry white wine
2 garlic cloves, crushed
1 fresh bay leaf
Pinch of saffron strands
Sprig of cilantro

To make marinade, mix together vinegar, wine, garlic, bay leaf, saffron and cilantro. Add pork and mix well to coat with marinade. Cover and leave in a cool place overnight. Remove pork with a slotted spoon and dry on paper towels. Reserve marinade.

Heat oil in a Dutch oven. Add onion and cook over low heat 5 minutes or until soft. Add pork and cook over high heat 10 minutes or until cooked through. Add strained marinade, tomato paste, salt and pepper and clams. Cover tightly and cook over a medium heat 5 minutes or until all clams have opened. Discard any that remain closed. Garnish with cilantro leaves and lemon wedges and serve.

Makes 4 to 6 servings.

SPANAKOPITTA

2/3 cup olive oil
1 onion, finely chopped
1 garlic clove, crushed
1 lb. frozen chopped spinach, thawed and well
   drained
2 tablespoons chopped fresh cilantro
1/2 teaspoon freshly grated nutmeg
4 oz. feta cheese, crumbled
1 cup curd cheese
Salt and freshly ground pepper
8 sheets filo pastry, about 16- x 12-inch
Cilantro leaves, to garnish

Preheat oven to 375F (190C). Brush a 12- x 9-inch baking sheet with oil.

Heat 2 tablespoons of oil in a skillet. Add onion and garlic and cook over low heat 5 minutes or until soft. Add spinach and cook, stirring, 2 minutes. Remove from heat and stir in cilantro, nutmeg, feta cheese, curd cheese, salt and pepper. Put 1 sheet of filo pastry on baking sheet. Brush pastry with oil and layer three more sheets on top, brushing each one with oil. Spread spinach mixture on top then cover with remaining pastry sheets, brushing each one with oil.

Trim overhanging pastry then tuck in edges to seal. Brush top with oil. With a sharp knife, cut through top layers to mark 16 squares. Cook in oven 30 minutes or until golden brown and crisp. Leave in pan 10 minutes, then cut into marked squares. Garnish with cilantro leaves and serve hot or warm.

Makes 16 squares.

CAPONATA

1/2 cup olive oil
1 onion, chopped
4 stalks celery, sliced
12 oz. tomatoes, peeled (page 17) and chopped
3 tablespoons balsamic vinegar
1 tablespoon sugar
2 eggplant, diced
1 tablespoon capers, drained
12 green olives, pitted and roughly chopped
1 tablespoon pine nuts, lightly toasted
Salt and freshly ground pepper
2 tablespoons chopped fresh basil
Red bell pepper strips and basil sprigs, to garnish

Heat 2 tablespoons of oil in a saucepan. Add onion and cook 5 minutes.

Add celery and cook 3 minutes. Stir in tomatoes and simmer, uncovered, 5 minutes. Add vinegar and sugar and simmer 15 minutes. Heat remaining oil in a large skillet and cook eggplant until tender and golden.

Remove with a slotted spoon and add to tomato sauce. Add capers, olives and pine nuts and season with salt and pepper. Simmer 2 or 3 minutes. Stir in basil, transfer to a serving dish and let cool. Garnish with bell pepper strips and basil sprigs and serve.

Makes 4 to 6 servings.

— CHAR-BROILED ARTICHOKES —

1/3 cup olive oil
1 garlic clove, crushed
2 tablespoons chopped fresh parsley
Salt and freshly ground pepper
6 baby artichokes
Flat-leaf parsley sprigs, to garnish
RED BELL PEPPER SAUCE:
1 tablespoon olive oil
1 small onion, chopped
2 red bell peppers, diced
1 cup vegetable stock

Mix together olive oil, garlic, parsley, salt and pepper. Set aside.

To make red bell pepper sauce, heat oil in a saucepan. Add onion and cook 5 minutes or until soft. Add red bell peppers and cook over low heat 5 minutes. Pour in stock, bring to a boil, reduce heat and simmer 10 minutes. Push through a sieve or puree in a food processor or blender. Season with salt and pepper.

Trim bases of artichokes and remove any tough outer leaves. Cut artichokes in half lengthwise and immediately brush with seasoned oil. Preheat a ridged broiler pan, add artichokes and cook over a medium heat 10 minutes, turning once, until browned on both sides. Reheat sauce. Drizzle artichokes with remaining seasoned oil, garnish with parsley and serve with red bell pepper sauce.

Makes 3 or 4 servings.

— POLENTA WITH VEGETABLES —

Salt and freshly ground pepper
Scant 1 cup polenta
1 tablespoon butter
1 small eggplant, thinly sliced
1 zucchini, thinly sliced
1/2 cup olive oil
1 red bell pepper, quartered
Basil sprigs, to garnish

Put 2-1/2 cups water in a saucepan and bring to a boil. Add a pinch of salt then pour in polenta in a fine, steady stream, stirring vigorously with a wooden spoon.

Simmer 5 to 10 minutes, stirring frequently, until polenta is thick and no longer grainy. Remove pan from heat and stir in butter and black pepper. Turn polenta on to an oiled baking sheet or wooden board and spread out to a thickness of 1/4 to 1/2 inch. Cool, cover and refrigerate 1 hour. With a 2-1/2- to 3-inch pastry cutter, cut into eight circles. Preheat broiler. Brush eggplant and zucchini with oil and broil until browned on both sides. Keep warm.

Broil bell pepper quarters and peel (page 28). Keep warm. Brush polenta circles with oil and broil 3 or 4 minutes on each side until browned and crisp. Place a polenta circle on each of four serving plates and arrange vegetable slices on top. Season with salt and pepper and top with a polenta circle. Garnish with basil and serve.

Makes 4 servings.

— EGGPLANT WITH SKORDALIA —

2 small eggplant, sliced
Oil for frying
BATTER:
1 cup all-purpose flour
Pinch of salt
2 tablespoons butter, melted
1 egg white
SKORDALIA:
3 garlic cloves, crushed
2-inch thick slice white bread
1-1/4 cups ground almonds
1/2 cup olive oil
2 teaspoons lemon juice

To make batter, sift flour and salt into a large bowl.

Add butter and 3/4 cup tepid water, beating to form a smooth cream. Let stand 1 hour. To make skordalia, put garlic in a food processor or blender. Remove crusts from bread. Squeeze bread in a little cold water, then add to garlic with ground almonds and a little olive oil. With motor running, gradually add remaining oil. Stir in lemon juice, salt and pepper.

Whisk egg white until stiff then fold into batter. Heat 1/2-inch oil in a skillet. Dip eggplant slices into batter. Fry, in batches, 4 minutes, turning once, until crisp and golden on both sides. Drain on paper towels and keep warm while frying remaining slices. Serve eggplant slices with skordalia.

Makes 4 servings.

– RATATOUILLE IN OLIVE TARTS –

1/4 cup olive oil
1 onion, chopped
1 garlic clove, crushed
1 eggplant, diced
1 zucchini, diced
1 red bell pepper, diced
3 tomatoes, peeled (page 17) and roughly chopped
1 teaspoon dried herbes de Provence
Salt and freshly ground pepper
Mint sprigs and endive leaves, to garnish
PASTRY:
2 cups all-purpose flour, sifted
1/2 cup butter
1 oz. black olives, pitted and roughly chopped
1 egg, beaten
1 tablespoon olive oil

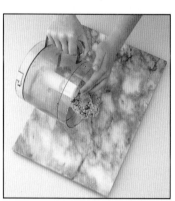

To make pastry, put flour, butter and a pinch of salt in a food processor and process until mixure resembles fine bread crumbs. Add olives and, with motor running, add egg and olive oil and process until mixture forms a ball. Remove from food processor. Wrap in plastic wrap and refrigerate 30 minutes.

Preheat oven to 400F (200C). Heat 2 tablespoons of olive oil in a skillet. Add onion and garlic and cook over low heat 5 minutes or until soft. Add eggplant, zucchini and bell pepper and cook 5 minutes.

Stir in tomatoes, herbes de Provence, salt and pepper. Cover and cook 10 minutes, stirring occasionally. Uncover and cook 15 minutes or until vegetables are tender but not too soft.

Meanwhile, prepare pastry cases. Thinly roll out pastry on a lightly floured surface. Cut out six circles of pastry to fit six 4-inch tartlet pans. Line pans with pastry, prick all over with a fork and press a square of foil into each one.

Bake pastry cases 15 minutes, then remove foil and bake another 10 to 15 minutes or until pastry is crisp. Reheat ratatouille, if necessary, and spoon into pastry cases. Drizzle with remaining olive oil, garnish with mint and endive leaves and serve.

Makes 6 servings.

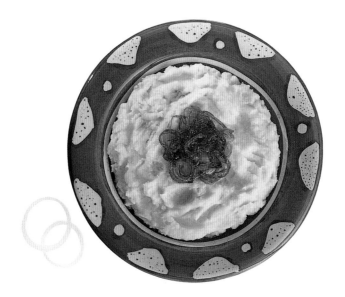

— GARLIC & OLIVE OIL MASH —

1 small garlic bulb
1lb. baking potatoes, cut into chunks
5 tablespoons extra-virgin olive oil
1/4 cup milk
Salt and freshly ground pepper
2 onions, finely sliced
1 tablespoon balsamic vinegar
1 tablespoon extra-virgin olive oil, to serve

Preheat oven to 400F (200C). Cut top off garlic bulb. Wrap garlic loosely in foil and cook in oven 20 to 30 minutes or until soft.

Cook potatoes in a saucepan of boiling salted water 15 to 20 minutes or until soft. Drain thoroughly and return to pan. Heat milk until warm. Squeeze soft garlic cloves out of their skins and add to potatoes. Mash potatoes. Gradually stir in 1/4 cup of oil, alternating with milk, until potatoes reach desired consistency. Season with salt and pepper.

Meanwhile, heat remaining oil in a skillet. Add onions and cook slowly, stirring frequently, 20 minutes or until soft and golden brown. Stir in balsamic vinegar. Top potatoes with fried onions, drizzle with olive oil and serve.

Makes 4 servings.

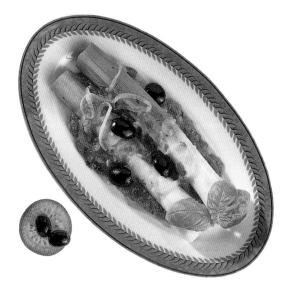

LEEKS NIÇOISE

1/4 cup olive oil
1 onion, thinly sliced
8 small leeks
3 tomatoes, peeled (page 17) and cut into eighths
1 garlic clove, crushed
1 tablespoon chopped fresh basil
1 tablespoon chopped fresh parsley
8 black olives, pitted and halved
Salt and freshly ground pepper
Basil sprigs, to garnish

Heat oil in a skillet. Add onion and cook 5 minutes or until soft. Add leeks and cook, turning, until just beginning to brown.

Add tomatoes. Stir in garlic, basil, parsley, olives, salt and pepper. Cover and cook over low heat 15 to 20 minutes or until leeks are tender, turning from time to time.

Remove leeks with a slotted spoon and transfer to a warmed serving dish. Boil sauce 1 or 2 minutes or until reduced and thickened. Pour over leeks. Garnish with basil and serve hot or at room temperature.

Makes 4 servings.

FENNEL SICILIANO

3 fennel bulbs
1 cup fresh bread crumbs
1 oz. pine nuts
1/4 cup raisins
1 teaspoon chopped fresh thyme
1/4 cup grated Parmesan cheese
1/4 cup olive oil
Salt and freshly ground pepper
Fennel leaves, to garnish

Preheat oven to 375F (190C). Trim fennel and discard outer leaves, if necessary. Quarter bulbs and thinly slice.

Bring a saucepan of salted water to a boil. Add fennel and simmer 3 to 5 minutes or until just soft. Drain thoroughly. Brush an ovenproof dish with olive oil and arrange fennel slices in it in an even layer.

Mix together bread crumbs, pine nuts, raisins, thyme, Parmesan, olive oil, salt and pepper. Sprinkle mixture over fennel, making sure raisins are beneath surface. Cook in oven 20 to 30 minutes, or until golden. Garnish with fennel leaves and serve.

Makes 4 servings.

SPINACH WITH RAISINS

1/3 cup raisins
2 lbs. young spinach leaves
1/4 cup olive oil
1 garlic clove, crushed
3 tablespoons pine nuts
Salt and freshly ground pepper
2 slices bread, crusts removed

Put raisins in a bowl and cover with boiling water. Set aside. Wash spinach and put in a saucepan with only water that clings to its leaves.

Cover and cook 2 or 3 minutes then drain thoroughly and chop roughly. Heat half oil in a large skillet. Add garlic and pine nuts and cook, stirring, 2 or 3 minutes or until pine nuts are golden all over.

Drain raisins and add to pan with spinach. Cook, stirring, 5 minutes. Season with salt and pepper. Cut bread into 1/2-inch cubes. Heat remaining oil in a skillet. Add bread and fry, stirring, until golden and crisp. Scatter croûtons over spinach and serve.

Makes 4 servings.

— BROAD BEANS WITH FETA —

12 oz. shelled broad beans or lima beans
2 oz. sun-dried tomatoes
4 oz. feta cheese
1 tablespoon olive oil
Grated zest of 1/2 lemon
Freshly ground pepper
Chopped fresh chives, to garnish

Bring a saucepan of salted water to a boil.
Add beans and cook 3 to 5 minutes or until
just tender. Drain well and transfer beans to
a bowl.

Cut sun-dried tomatoes into small pieces.
Roughly crumble feta cheese.

Quickly toss together beans, sun-dried
tomatoes, feta cheese, olive oil, lemon zest
and black pepper. Transfer to a serving dish,
garnish with chives and serve immediately.

Makes 4 servings.

OKRA & TOMATOES

1 lb. small okra
1/4 cup olive oil
1 small onion, chopped
1 small leek, chopped
1 lb. tomatoes, peeled (page 17) and chopped
1 oz. sun-dried tomatoes, chopped
1 garlic clove, crushed
1 tablespoon lemon juice
1 teaspoon sugar
Salt and freshly ground pepper
Oregano leaves, to garnish

Cut stalks off okra but do not pierce pods. Wash pods, drain and pat dry.

Heat oil in a large skillet. Add onion and leek and cook 7 minutes or until softened and lightly coloured. Add okra and turn carefully to coat in oil. Cook 5 minutes.

Add tomatoes, sun-dried tomatoes, garlic, lemon juice, sugar, salt and pepper. Cover pan and simmer 10 minutes. Remove lid and cook 10 minutes or until okra is tender and sauce reduced and thickened. If sauce reduces too quickly, add a little water. Garnish with oregano leaves and serve hot or warm.

Makes 4 servings.

— GREEK BROILED VEGETABLES —

2 baby eggplant
4 baby zucchini
1 red bell pepper
1 yellow bell pepper
1 fennel bulb
4oz. feta cheese
1 tablespoon lemon juice
Salt and freshly ground pepper
Zucchini flowers, to garnish
MARINADE:
2/3 cup olive oil
2 garlic cloves, crushed
1 teaspoon chopped fresh parsley
1 teaspoon chopped fresh mint
1 teaspoon chopped fresh oregano

To make marinade, mix together olive oil, garlic, parsley, mint and oregano. Cut eggplant and zucchini lengthwise in half. Cut bell peppers into quarters and remove seeds. Quarter and slice fennel. Cut feta into small cubes and place in a bowl. Add a little marinade and mix gently. Put vegetables in another bowl with remaining marinade, mix together and leave 1 hour.

Preheat broiler or grill. Broil vegetables, turning and brushing with marinade every few minutes, 10 minutes, or until tender and flecked with brown. Let cool. Arrange vegetables on a serving plate. Drizzle with lemon juice and season with salt and pepper. Scatter feta on top, garnish with zucchini flowers and serve.

Makes 4 servings.

— TUNISIAN ORANGE SALAD —

4 small oranges
1 daikon
Mint sprigs, to garnish
DRESSING:
1 tablespoon lemon juice
2 teaspoons orange-flower water
1 teaspoon sugar
1/4 cup olive oil
Salt and freshly ground pepper
1 tablespoon chopped fresh mint

Cut peel off oranges, removing all pith. Thinly slice oranges.

Peel daikon and thinly slice. Arrange orange and daikon slices on a large serving plate. To make dressing, whisk together lemon juice, orange-flower water, sugar, olive oil, salt and pepper.

Pour dressing over orange and daikon slices. Sprinkle with chopped mint and refrigerate. Garnish with mint sprigs and serve.

Makes 4 servings.

Note: A daikon is a large white radish. If it is unavailable, this salad is also delicious made with sliced fennel.

– MOROCCAN BEETROOT SALAD –

2 lbs. raw beetroot
1 red onion, finely chopped
2 garlic cloves, finely chopped
4 ripe tomatoes
1 tablespoon chopped fresh cilantro
1 tablespoon chopped fresh parsley
Black olives, to garnish
DRESSING:
2 tablespoons balsamic vinegar
1/2 cup olive oil
1/2 teaspoon harissa
Salt and freshly ground pepper

Trim ends off beetroot. Cook in boiling salted water 1 hour until tender.

Drain and remove skins under cold running water. Thinly slice beetroot and put in a bowl. Scatter onion and garlic over. To make dressing, whisk together vinegar, olive oil, harissa, salt and pepper. Pour half dressing over warm beetroot mixture and mix gently.

Thinly slice tomatoes and put in a bowl. Add remaining dressing and mix gently. Arrange tomatoes around outside of a shallow serving dish and arrange beetroot in center. Scatter with chopped cilantro and parsley, garnish with black olives and serve.

Makes 4 to 6 servings.

COUSCOUS SALAD

2/3 cup quick-cook couscous
1 fresh red chile
8 oz. cherry tomatoes
1 bunch green onions
1/4 cup extra-virgin olive oil
2 tablespoons lemon juice
1/4 cup chopped fresh parsley
1/4 cup chopped fresh cilantro
Salt and freshly ground pepper
Salad greens, to serve

Put couscous in a bowl and add 2/3 cup cold water. Leave 30 to 60 minutes or until water has been completely absorbed.

Meanwhile, cut chile in half and remove core and seeds. Finely chop chile. Cut cherry tomatoes in half and slice green onions. Gently fluff up couscous with a fork.

Add olive oil, lemon juice, parsley, cilantro, salt and pepper to couscous. Gently stir in chile, tomatoes and green onions. Let stand 1 hour. Line a serving dish with salad greens, pile couscous in center and serve.

Makes 4 servings.

— CHICKPEA & ROCKET SALAD —

1 cup chickpeas, soaked overnight
1/4 cup olive oil
1 garlic clove, crushed
1 tablespoon ground cumin
2 teaspoons balsamic vinegar
1 small red onion, chopped
Salt and freshly ground pepper
1-1/2 oz. rocket
Red onion rings and rocket leaves, to garnish

Drain chickpeas, put in a saucepan and cover with cold water. Bring to a boil and boil rapidly 10 minutes. Reduce heat, cover and simmer 1 to 1-1/2 hours or until tender.

Heat olive oil in a skillet. Add garlic and cumin and cook over low heat, stirring, 2 or 3 minutes. Drain chickpeas and transfer to a bowl. Add warm oil, garlic and cumin mixture. Add balsamic vinegar, onion, salt and pepper. Mix gently and let cool.

Roughly chop rocket and stir gently into chickpeas. Garnish with red onion rings and rocket leaves and serve.

Makes 4 servings.

– LAVENDER HONEY ICE CREAM –

5 sprigs lavender flowers
2-1/2 cups milk
6 oz. lavender honey
4 egg yolks
2/3 cup whipping cream
2/3 cup crème fraîche
Lavender flowers, to decorate

Turn freezer to its coldest setting. Put lavender sprigs and milk in a saucepan and heat to almost boiling. Remove from heat and discard lavender sprigs.

Heat honey in a small saucepan until just melted. Whisk egg yolks in a large bowl until thick and foamy. Gradually whisk melted honey into egg yolks. Bring milk back to a boil. Pour on boiling milk, whisking constantly. Put bowl over a pan of simmering water. Heat, stirring, about 8 minutes or until mixture is thick enough to coat back of spoon. Strain into a bowl, cover and let cool. Stir in cream and crème fraîche.

Pour mixture into a freezerproof container. Put in freezer. When sides are beginning to set, transfer to a bowl and beat thoroughly or process in a food processor or blender. Return to container and freeze 30 to 40 minutes. When ice cream is just beginning to solidify, transfer to a bowl and beat again. Return to freezer until firm. Transfer to refrigerator 20 minutes before serving. Decorate with lavender flowers and serve.

Makes 4 to 6 servings.

PISTACHIO ICE CREAM

2 cups roasted pistachio nuts
1 cup sugar
4 egg yolks
2 cups full-fat milk
1-1/4 cups whipping cream
1/2 cup regular plain yogurt
Roughly chopped pistachio nuts, to decorate
Quartered figs, to serve

Turn freezer to its coldest setting. In a food processor, finely grind pistachio nuts with 1 tablespoon of sugar.

Whisk egg yolks and remaining sugar in a large bowl until thick and foamy. Put pistachio nuts, milk and cream in a small saucepan and bring to a boil. Pour on to egg yolk mixture, whisking constantly. Put bowl over a pan of simmering water. Heat, stirring, about 8 minutes, or until mixture is thick enough to coat back of spoon. Cover and let cool. Stir in yogurt.

Pour mixture into a freezerproof container. Put in freezer. When sides are beginning to set, transfer to a bowl and beat thoroughly or process in a food processor or blender. Return to container and freeze 30 to 40 minutes. When ice cream is just beginning to solidify, transfer to a bowl and beat again. Return to freezer until firm. Transfer to refrigerator 20 minutes before serving. Decorate with pistachios and serve with figs.

Makes 4 to 6 servings.

—— POMEGRANATE SORBET ——

1 cup granulated sugar
4 to 6 large pomegranates
Grated zest and juice of 1/2 orange
Grated zest and juice of 1/2 lemon
1 egg white
Pomegranate seeds and mint sprigs, to decorate

Turn freezer to its coldest setting. Put sugar and 1-1/4 cups water in a saucepan. Heat gently until sugar has dissolved then bring to a boil, reduce heat and simmer 5 minutes. Let cool. Cut pomegranates in half.

Squeeze pomegranates on a lemon squeezer to give 1-3/4 cups juice. Strain pomegranate juice into cooled syrup. Stir in orange and lemon zest and juice. Pour into a freezerproof container. Put in freezer. When sides are beginning to set, transfer to a bowl and beat thoroughly or process in a food processor or blender. Return to container and freeze 30 to 40 minutes.

When sorbet is just beginning to solidify, whisk egg white until stiff. Beat sorbet again until smooth. Fold in egg white. Return to freezer until firm. Transfer sorbet to refrigerator 20 minutes before serving. Decorate with pomegranate seeds and mint sprigs and serve.

Makes 4 to 6 servings.

— MOROCCAN RICE PUDDING —

1/2 cup short-grain rice
2-1/2 cups milk
Strip of orange peel
1/4 cup sugar
1/2 cup ground almonds
2 teaspoons orange-flower water
Ground cinnamon and toasted flaked almonds, to
  decorate
Sliced oranges, to serve

Rinse rice and put in a bowl with 1/2 cup water. Put milk and orange peel in a saucepan and bring to a boil.

Add sugar and stir until it has dissolved. Add rice and water. Cover and simmer 30 to 40 minutes or until most of liquid has been absorbed.

Add ground almonds and cook, stirring, 2 or 3 minutes. Stir in orange-flower water. Spoon into serving dishes and let cool. Decorate with ground cinnamon and flaked almonds and serve with sliced oranges.

Makes 4 servings.

– AMARETTI-STUFFED PEACHES –

4 large peaches
2 oz. amaretti biscuits
1 egg yolk
4 teaspoons sugar
2 tablespoons softened butter
1 cup sweet white wine
Toasted flaked almonds and vine leaves, to decorate

Preheat oven to 375F (190C). Butter an ovenproof dish. Cut peaches in half and remove pits.

Scoop out a little flesh from each peach half and place in a bowl. Crush amaretti biscuits and add to bowl. Stir in egg yolk, sugar and butter and mix well. Put some filling in each peach half, forming it into a smooth mound.

Put peaches in dish and pour in wine. Cook in oven 30 to 40 minutes or until peaches are tender and filling is firm. Transfer to serving plates, sprinkle with toasted almonds and decorate with vine leaves. Spoon cooking juices around and serve.

Makes 4 servings.

Note: Be careful not to cook peaches for too long - they should retain their shape.

PEARS IN RED WINE

4 ripe but firm pears
2-1/2 cups red wine
2 tablespoons sugar
2-inch piece cinnamon stick
Pared zest of 1/2 lemon
2 tablespoons crème de cassis
Toasted brioche slices, to serve

Peel pears, keeping them whole and leaving stalks on.

Put wine and sugar in a large, heavy-bottomed saucepan and heat gently until dissolved. Add cinnamon stick and lemon zest. Put pears side by side in saucepan. Bring to a boil, reduce heat, cover and simmer 15 minutes or until pears are tender, turning pears once and basting with cooking liquid from time to time.

Remove with a slotted spoon and place on a serving dish. Add crème de cassis to cooking liquid and boil a few minutes or until syrupy. Discard cinnamon stick and lemon zest and spoon syrup over pears. Serve warm or refrigerated with toasted brioche slices.

Makes 4 servings.

Note: If crème de cassis is not available it may be omitted from recipe.

DRIED FRUIT SALAD

2/3 cup orange juice
1/3 cup light brown sugar
1 tablespoon orange liqueur
2-1/4 cups mixed dried fruit, eg apricots, peaches,
   pitted dates, figs, pears
1/3 cup raisins
1/4 cup blanched almonds
1 tablespoon chopped pistachio nuts
Regular plain yogurt and ground cinnamon, to serve

Put orange juice in a saucepan and heat until
warm. Add sugar and heat, stirring, until
dissolved.

Remove from heat and stir in orange liqueur
and 3/4 cup cold water. Add mixed fruit,
raisins and orange juice mixture. Turn fruit
in liquid. Transfer to a bowl and add more
water, if necessary, to cover.

Cover bowl and leave in a cool place 24
hours. Add almonds and pistachio nuts and
stir to mix with fruit. Serve with yogurt,
sprinkled with cinnamon.

Makes 4 servings.

ROAST FIGS

12 figs
3 tablespoons sugar
1 tablespoon orange juice
2/3 cup walnut halves
1 tablespoon honey
Regular plain yogurt, to serve

Preheat oven to 400F (200C). Butter a shallow flameproof dish. Put figs side by side in dish.

Sprinkle with 2 tablespoons of sugar and orange juice. Cook in oven 20 minutes, basting from time to time with cooking juices. Add walnuts and sprinkle with remaining sugar.

Reduce oven temperature to 300F (150C) and cook another 10 minutes. Remove figs and walnuts with a slotted spoon and arrange on a serving dish. Add honey to cooking juices and warm through over low heat. Spoon syrup over figs and serve warm or cold with yogurt.

Makes 4 servings.

— ORANGE & ALMOND CAKE —

1/2 cup butter
Grated zest of 1 orange
1/2 cup sugar
2 eggs, beaten
1 cup semolina
1 cup ground almonds
1 teaspoon baking powder
3 tablespoons orange juice
Strips of pared orange zest, to decorate
SYRUP:
1 cup orange juice
1/2 cup sugar
2 teaspoons orange-flower water

Preheat oven to 350F (180C). Butter and line bottom of an 8-inch cake pan.

Beat together butter, orange zest and sugar until light and creamy. Gradually beat in eggs. Mix together semolina, ground almonds and baking powder and fold half into creamed mixture with half orange juice. Fold in remaining semolina mixture and orange juice. Spoon mixture into prepared pan and bake 30 to 40 minutes or until well risen - a skewer inserted into center should come out clean.

Let cool in pan a few minutes. Meanwhile, make syrup. Put orange juice and sugar in a saucepan. Heat gently until sugar has dissolved. Bring to a boil, reduce heat and simmer 4 minutes. Stir in orange-flower water. Turn cake out on to a deep serving plate and spoon syrup on top. Decorate with orange zest and serve warm or cold.

Makes 8 servings.

— CLEMENTINE & DATE SALAD —

8 clementines
2 teaspoons orange-flower water
3/4 cup dates
1/4 cup pistachio nuts
Clementine leaves, to decorate

Peel clementines. Cut them into slices, reserving any juice.

Arrange clementine slices on serving plates. Add reserved juice and sprinkle with orange-flower water.

Remove pits from dates. Chop dates. Roughly chop pistachio nuts. Scatter dates and nuts over clementines. Decorate with clementine leaves and serve.

Makes 4 to 6 servings.

SAFFRON NECTARINES

4 ripe nectarines
1 tablespoon butter
1/4 cup clear blossom honey
Pinch of saffron strands
1 tablespoon rosewater
Toasted flaked almonds, to decorate

Cut nectarines in half and remove pits. Put nectarine halves in a saucepan with butter.

Spoon honey over and scatter with saffron. Add 1/2 cup water and rosewater. Bring slowly to a boil, reduce heat and simmer 8 to 12 minutes or until nectarines are tender.

Remove with a slotted spoon and arrange on serving plates. Decorate with toasted flaked almonds and serve warm or cold.

Makes 4 servings.

SERPENT CAKE

Powdered sugar for dusting
12 sheets filo pastry, about 16- x 12-inch
1/3 cup unsalted butter, melted
Ground cinnamon, to decorate
ALMOND PASTE:
2 cups ground almonds
3/4 cup powdered sugar
Grated zest and juice of 1/2 orange
1/4 cup softened butter

To make almond paste, mix together ground almonds, powdered sugar, orange zest, orange juice and butter. Cover and refrigerate 30 minutes, or until firm.

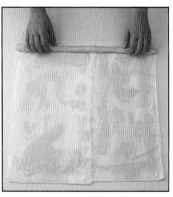

Preheat oven to 350F (180C). Dust a work surface with powdered sugar. Divide almond paste into three and roll each piece into a sausage 20-inch long. Brush two sheets of filo pastry with melted butter and place side by side, with long sides overlapping slightly. Place two more buttered sheets on top. Lay a roll of almond paste along one of long sides and roll up. Brush with butter and roll into a tight coil. Place coil on a baking sheet.

Make two more rolls in same way. Join them to coil, continuing shape and sealing joins with water. Bake 20 to 30 minutes or until crisp and golden. Invert on to another baking sheet and return to oven until crisp. Invert on to a serving dish and let cool. Dust with powdered sugar. Decorate with stripes of ground cinnamon and serve.

Makes 6 servings.

Note: This cake does not keep well and is best eaten on day it is made.

CANDIED FRUIT TARTS

1 cup ricotta cheese
3 egg yolks
1/4 cup sugar
1 tablespoon brandy
Grated zest of 1 lemon
1 tablespoon lemon juice
4 oz. crystallized fruit, finely chopped
Powdered sugar for dusting
Mint sprigs, to decorate
PASTRY:
1-1/2 cups all-purpose flour
1/3 cup butter
1/3 cup shortening

To make pastry, sift flour into a bowl. Add butter and shortening.

Rub in butter and shortening until mixture resembles fine bread crumbs. Stir in 2 tablespoons of cold water and use a knife to mix to a smooth dough. Knead lightly, wrap in plastic wrap and refrigerate 30 minutes. Preheat oven to 350F (180C). On a lightly floured surface, roll out pastry until 1/8-inch thick. Cut out four circles to fit four 4-inch tart pans.

Put ricotta cheese, egg yolks, sugar, brandy and lemon zest and juice in a bowl. Beat together until smooth then stir in crystallized fruit. Divide mixture among pastry cases. Bake 30 to 40 minutes or until filling is set and golden. Let cool. Dust with powdered sugar, decorate with mint sprigs and serve cold.

Makes 4 servings.

FIG & ORANGE TART

8oz. no-soak dried figs, roughly chopped
Juice of 2 oranges
1/3 cup butter, diced
2 eggs, beaten
2 tablespoons pine nuts
Powdered sugar for dusting
Orange segments, to decorate
PASTRY:
1-1/4 cups all-purpose flour
1/3 cup butter
2 tablespoons powdered sugar
1 egg yolk

To make pastry, sift flour into a bowl. Rub in butter until mixture resembles fine bread crumbs.

Stir in powdered sugar. Add egg yolk and 1 teaspoon of water. Stir with a knife to form a smooth dough. Knead lightly, wrap in plastic wrap and refrigerate 30 minutes. On a lightly floured surface, roll out dough to fit a 8-inch loose-bottomed tart pan. Line tart pan with pastry and refrigerate again 20 to 30 minutes. Preheat oven to 375F (190C). Prick pastry all over with a fork then line with foil and fill with baking beans. Bake blind 10 to 15 minutes or until pastry has set.

Remove baking beans and foil and bake another 10 to 15 minutes or until firm and golden brown. Put figs and orange juice in a saucepan. Cook 5 to 10 minutes, stirring, until thickened. Remove from heat, add butter and stir until melted. Beat in eggs. Pour mixture into pastry case and scatter with pine nuts. Bake 15 minutes or until just set. Dust with powdered sugar, decorate with orange segments and serve warm or cold.

Makes 6 servings.

FRUIT & NUT BAKLAVA

3/4 cup finely chopped walnuts
1/4 cup pistachio nuts, finely chopped
1/3 cup sultanas
1/2 cup no-soak dried apricots, chopped
1 teaspoon ground cinnamon
2 tablespoons light brown sugar
5 sheets filo pastry, about 16- x 12-inch
1/3 cup unsalted butter, melted
Mint sprigs, to decorate
SYRUP:
2/3 cup granulated sugar
1 tablespoon lemon juice
Pared zest of 1 orange

Mix together walnuts, pistachio nuts, sultanas, apricots, cinnamon and sugar.

Preheat oven to 325F (160C). Cut pastry sheets crosswise in half. Brush a 11- x 8-inch baking pan with melted butter. Brush one pastry sheet with butter and put in pan. Layer three more sheets on top, brushing each with butter. Spread half nut mixture on top. Cover with two more layers of buttered pastry. Spread over remaining nut mixture. Top with remaining buttered pastry. Trim edges of pastry. Score top pastry layer in three lines lengthwise then score diagonal lines about 1-inch apart, to make diamonds.

Bake 25 minutes. Increase oven temperature to 425F (220C) and bake 5 to 10 minutes or until golden brown. Just before end of cooking time, make syrup. Put sugar in a small saucepan with 6 tablespoons water, lemon juice and pared orange zest. Heat gently until sugar dissolves then bring to a boil and boil 5 minutes. Strain hot syrup over hot baklava. Let cool then cut into diamonds, decorate with mint and serve.

Makes approximately 20 diamonds.

INDEX